INVOKE
THE
GODDESS

About the Author

A lifelong student of the Mysteries and practitioner of conscious connection with the Divine, Kala Trobe is thoroughly enjoying this era of ever-increasing awareness of the sanctity of all life and its infinite potential. She paints and writes on such themes as spiritual evolution, goddesses, and magicks. She also reads tarot professionally, celebrates diversity, and loves languages, insightful literature, travel, and cats.

To Write to the Author

If you wish to contact the author or would like more information about this book, please write to the author in care of Llewellyn Worldwide Ltd. and we will forward your request. Both the author and publisher appreciate hearing from you and learning of your enjoyment of this book and how it has helped you. Llewellyn Worldwide Ltd. cannot guarantee that every letter written to the author can be answered, but all will be forwarded. Please write to:

Kala Trobe
℅ Llewellyn Worldwide
2143 Wooddale Drive
Woodbury, MN 55125-2989

Please enclose a self-addressed stamped envelope for reply,
or $1.00 to cover costs. If outside the U.S.A., enclose
an international postal reply coupon.

Many of Llewellyn's authors have websites with additional
information and resources. For more information,
please visit our website at http://www.llewellyn.com.

INVOKE
THE
GODDESS

Connecting
to the
Hindu, Greek,
& Egyptian
Deities

KALA TROBE

Llewellyn Publications
Woodbury, Minnesota

SECOND EDITION, Revised
First Printing, 2019
First Edition, 2 printings

Book design by Samantha Penn
Cover design by Shira Atakpu
Interior Art by Kate Thomssen

Llewellyn Publications is a registered trademark of Llewellyn Worldwide Ltd.

Library of Congress Cataloging-in-Publication Data
Names: Trobe, Kala, author.
Title: Invoke the goddess : connecting to the Hindu, Greek, and Egyptian
    deities / Kala Trobe.
Description: Second edition. | Woodbury, Minnesota : Llewellyn Publications, [2019]
    | Includes bibliographical references.
Identifiers: LCCN 2019011663 (print) | LCCN 2019014980 (ebook) | ISBN
    9780738759647 (ebook) | ISBN 9780738759623 (alk. paper)
Subjects: LCSH: Hindu goddesses—Miscellanea. | Goddesses,
    Egyptian—Miscellanea. | Goddesses, Greek—Miscellanea. |
    Invocation—Miscellanea.
Classification: LCC BF1623.G63 (ebook) | LCC BF1623.G63 T76 2019 (print) |
    DDC 133.9—dc23
LC record available at https://lccn.loc.gov/2019011663

Llewellyn Worldwide Ltd. does not participate in, endorse, or have any authority or responsibility concerning private business transactions between our authors and the public.

All mail addressed to the author is forwarded but the publisher cannot, unless specifically instructed by the author, give out an address or phone number.

Any internet references contained in this work are current at publication time, but the publisher cannot guarantee that a specific location will continue to be maintained. Please refer to the publisher's website for links to authors' websites and other sources.

Llewellyn Publications
A Division of Llewellyn Worldwide Ltd.
2143 Wooddale Drive
Woodbury, MN 55125-2989
www.llewellyn.com

Printed in the United States of America

Other Books by Kala Trobe

Invoke the Gods

Magic of Qabalah

The Witch's Guide to Life

The Magick Bookshop

Magick in the West End

How to Find Your Inner Priestess

The Little Book of Pocket Spells (as Akasha Moon)

Ascension (a novel)

Spiritus (a novel)

*The Mystical and the Mundane in the
Works of John Cowper Powys*

*Dedicated on a wave of frankincense and patchouli oil
to Geraldine Chelvaiyah, née White, 12/04/49 to 13/10/2018,
daughter of Isis much loved and missed; and to Roxy, Sophia, and Isla*

CONTENTS

Part III: Greek Goddesses

Contents

INTRODUCTION

INVOKE THE GODDESS IS a magickal workbook. It is designed to enable the reader to access and channel specific goddess wavelengths. By interacting with these deities and maintaining a strong inner will, it becomes possible to gain blessings and insight, to influence the psychic space in which we exist, and thus to alter personal circumstance.

With the goal of individual gnosis in mind, and in order to attain specific practical results, five goddesses have been selected from each of three major religious backgrounds: Hindu, Egyptian, and Greek. The exercises and visualizations allow one to access these deities on a personally interactive as well as a cosmic level. Each goddess offers properties and experiences applicable to our physical, emotional, and spiritual lives.

That positive visualization can bring positive results is a fact widely heralded, and an underlying principle of this book. However, the visualization processes described within are no mere placebos; the godforms involved are intelligent entities and interaction with them may take place in what seems to be the imagination, but it is not imaginary. As anyone who has practiced such meditations and bhaktis will confirm, the deities, whether they start on the earth plane as statues, images, symbols, or focused thoughts, very soon take on a life of their own, and the results inevitably filter down to the material planes.

Equally real is the effect of these encounters on one's psychology. The visualizations lead the participant into a direct encounter with a powerful archetypal deity, whose symbols and presence will make a profound impression on the subconscious, stimulating one's innate capacity for self-healing and self-development. The same applies to the visualizations for specific goals, such as acquiring a long-term partner or attaining prosperity; not only does a seeker appeal to a relevant deity, but one's higher self is brought into action, aiding that process: "The gods help those who help themselves."

Also included are exercises designed to help seekers delve in a controlled manner into the murkier areas of their psyche and, with the aid of a divinity, bring conflicting currents to check; or, even better, to harness these disturbances and "negative" experiences as a creative and evolutionary energy source. These qualities are particularly available through the more challenging goddesses such as Kali, Sekhmet, and aspects of Hecate. Sometimes it becomes crucial to look into the painful darkness of our own fears and faults before we can experience a trusting deliverance into the light.

These inner journeys are described step by step as far as is possible without subjecting the psychic voyager to a contrived experience. Room has been left for personal extrapolation, while every effort has been made to aid creative thinking and to provide enough signposts to keep the seeker on the right path. However, preset routes are by their nature far from definitive, and seekers are encouraged to use their own judgment and interpret them accordingly. Personal encounters are always more relevant than second-hand knowledge, though the latter is helpful in guiding us to the relevant area of the universal psyche. These experiences are, after all, archetypal, and subsequently par-sculpted by all who have undergone them. Because such a clear subconscious map exists in our astral and etheric DNA, it is very safe to use one's intuition in these exercises. In so doing, one is accessing wisdom far greater than that normally made available to us.

These exercises are intended to create intense and transformative states in the user. Their aim is predominantly healing and magickal elevation, enhancement of quality of life, and reconnection with spiritual Source.

How to Perform the Visualizations

There are several ways to approach these visualizations. Many of the exercises are performed by candlelight and involve meditative states, and some readers may prefer a ritualistic approach, but this by no means excludes the possibility of simply visualizing while reading the exercises. Indeed, this can be very powerful, particularly if done in a state of heightened emotion. Additionally, every chapter begins with a section of poetic prose specifically designed to stimulate the imagination and open it out toward that particular goddess. For some, focused reading alone will be enough to set the magick rolling.

A few years ago, for example, I heard from a man who declared himself a former cynic, now converted to a wider awareness. *Invoke the Goddess* in its original form had landed in his vicinity via a family member at a time when he was due to interview for a job he particularly wanted, and it caught his eye. Considering nothing ventured, nothing gained, he decided to try a new approach. After consulting the index of goddess functions, he went to the Lakshmi section and found the exercise most appropriate to his cause: for spiritual and material well-being. In a quiet space, he cleared his mind, and in his own time went through the mental processes described. Unversed in any yogic practices and not keen on candles, incense, or mantras, he simply focused and strongly visualized whilst reading the text. A suitable state thus attained, I am thrilled to say he got and kept the job. The moral of this story is to do what feels best for you and do it your own way.

I too have often had powerful experiences while simply reading and strongly imagining rituals or magickal techniques, often also by writing them down. A great deal can be achieved on the astral/spiritual planes while the body remains relatively immobile, a principle that underlines all of these visualizations. We each have our favored approaches to supplication and worship with its many ramifications, some active and demonstrative, while others may find gestures, chanting aloud, and so on to be distracting. This book provides for all attitudes and gives ideas rather than rules.

If you prefer not to punctuate your meditation by referring to the book, one option is to familiarize yourself with the "route" beforehand. Memorize the major symbols or make bullet-point notes and capture the essence of the goddess by reading the sections describing her personality and functions.

Once you have committed the exercise to memory or summed it up handily, you should be able to perform it while in a relaxed, meditative state.

Another possibility is to have a friend or partner read the exercise aloud while you visualize it. This can also be done in group situations with one person reading and the rest taking the inner journey. This of course has the added advantage of enabling participants to exchange experiences and information afterward if so desired.

Finally, you could record yourself reading the exercise and leave suitable space to accomplish the various stages of the meditation. This allows you to be absolutely relaxed when the visualization is performed and drift off into inner space with no holds barred. A couple of attempts at this will enable you to assess your time requirements at each stage.

Like every living thing (whether apparently so or not—think trees, rivers, mineral formations), god- and goddess-forms are intelligent patterns of energy, albeit particularly refined and powerful ones. They are entities full of personality and sacredness, perhaps elevated into a prolonged and enhanced existence by the intense and continual input of other beings, perhaps entirely independent. Some developed from and provided the atavistic necessities of the species, such as light and warmth (solar and fire deities) and food (gods of hunting and harvest); others have brought forth and grown from civilization, such as gods of intellect and artistry. Myth attempts to project inner reality onto a cosmic screen as well as to describe the nature of our arrival at consciousness.

Not only are the gods and goddesses at large on the astral and spiritual/causal planes, they are also in our very midst every day. I do not mean courtesy of psychic perception alone, but as psychological archetypes alive in us all in some shape, form, or mixture; usually the latter. As many a witch or spiritual psychologist knows, it is great fun to spot the Ancient Ones wandering through our lives in an often quite blatant manner as nomadic archetypes, and these can provide us with valuable psychotherapeutic clues as to our nature and needs. More and more of the godforms are making themselves known in this manner; the age-old constellations of consciousness are comprehensively spangling our inner space.

❧

The rise in popularity over the last decades of many ancient pantheons reflects a modern need to reclaim personal interaction with both the natural world and the divine. It expresses a global desire for deities of specific function and form unavailable in most orthodox religions. No longer is a clergical intercessor required to create or sanctify one's connection with Source: a huge advantage of the current occidental era is that the God(dess) has now become personal. Of course, in some venerable religions such as Hinduism, particularly Advaita, this has long been the case, with the divine by its very nature being everywhere rather than made manifest exclusively inside a human-made building or via a ministry in a preapproved context. In general, however, independent spirituality has been anathema. It is a huge privilege to be present in a time and place in which personal mystical experience within the belief system of one's own choice is possible, legal, and no longer unusual. Channeling and/or interacting with the divine has consequently never been freer or more socially acceptable.

That being said, I am a firm believer in discretion when discussing or revealing one's personal spirituality and magicks. With so much dependent on the perceptions and preconceived notions of the listener, an authentic experience can easily be sullied by their doubt, disbelief, envy, or even laughter. Casually talking of, or portentously announcing, even small psychic interactions can provoke misunderstanding, prideful self-delusion, and apparent boastfulness, and is likely to dissipate the positive import and authenticity of the interaction. Harken ye well unto the powers of the Sphinx: "To Know, to Will, to Dare, and to Keep Silent!"

The practitioner may benefit from attunement to astrological specifics when deciding when to perform the visualizations or by picking a day or date that relates to that deity to aid the vibrations, although this is not a necessity. Moon phases are key to any spell and will likely prove relevant; seasons and their flora and symbols are also referenced alongside the exercises where significant.

Keeping a fast prior to the visualizations is a bonus, as is restraint from any negative indulgences. The eating of meat is anathema to most spiritual practices for numerous reasons. Please bear in mind which deities you are dealing with: it would be vile, for example, to approach a Hindu god or goddess, to whom the cow (Gau) is most sacred, with beef on your breath or in your gut. Likewise would it be counterintuitive to approach those bastions of justice and temperance, Ma'at or Iris, while tipsy or high. Common-sense awareness should allow you to deduce these important aspects of courtesy and taboo.

Washing before ritual is of huge benefit: see the next section.

All of this being said, the most essential factors are an open heart and mind.

Once your celestial interchange has been established, thank the Goddess and offer gifts as seems apt to you: a flame, incense, a flower, or more elaborate offerings. Afterward, allow the deity to "depart" before you do. Otherwise, just go with the sacred flow!

Ritual Baths

Ritual baths or lustrations are an excellent preliminary to any magickal endeavor, creating a suitable atmosphere and relaxing body and mind alike. It is traditional, of course, to make ablutions before worship and ritual in almost all cultures. Modern takes on this theme range from simple salt baths to elaborate psychic consommés, and a recipe appropriate to the individual goddess is given prior to most of the meditations.

In addition to the herbs and essential oils traditionally used in bathing waters, gemstones may be added to cold water and left for a while to imbue it with their specific qualities. Rose quartz, for example, exudes positive, compassionate properties that are of great use when dealing with hurt feelings and the cosmic chill of lack of faith. A quantity may be left to soak in water, and the water then poured into the bath in conjunction with rose oil and perhaps some pink solarized or "Aura-Soma"–style water. The person who steps into this bath is unlikely to remain unhappy for long.

Color-treated water is particularly good to use in the ritual bath; it strengthens chakras and aids with visualizing them. However, use natural dyes from flowers, spices, herbs, and barks, and in moderation so as not to tint or irritate the skin. Never use chemical colorings. Alternatively, you can simply visualize the color suffusing the water before you step into it.

Candles around the bathtub also create a wonderful ambience. Their colors may be chosen with a specific aim or chakra area in mind.

A Brief Guide to Color Usage

Red: Strength, determination, passion, sex

Yellow: Emotional healing, health, financial prosperity, intellect

Orange: Vitality, happiness, antidepressive

Green: New beginnings, balance, growth, fertility, financial prosperity

Pale Pink: Comfort, love, affection, heart-mender

Dark Pink: Fun, challenge, adventure, feisty frolickings, sex, beauty

Blue: Calming, inspiring; poetic inspiration

Violet: Spirituality, inner vision, psychic development

Purple: Akasha (deep spiritual knowledge), high ritual; spiritual, physical, and/or emotional self-sacrifice

Black: Self-protection, attack, vengeance, curse-making and breaking, powerful psychological changes

Turquoise: Self-defense, both psychic and physical; attunement to the cosmic will in action

Chakras

There are many detailed books as well as free online articles and lectures on the complex subject of auras and chakras; the newcomer is advised to purchase or watch one. Opinions vary as to some chakric associations and properties, largely due to the conflict between traditional Hindu-Buddhist symbolism and modern interpretations of the chakras. For the sake of clarity, in this book I have adhered to the Westernized version, which allies the chakras with the colors of the spectrum and makes them simple and effective to visualize; however, the arcane symbols and colors may be of more relevance to some readers. It is good to experiment in both schools of thought in order to deepen understanding and to find which feels best for you.

A chart or banner depicting the chakras in order will provide an invaluable mental map of the psychic bodies; keeping one in the room in which you meditate can be very useful.

The Sanskrit word *chakra* means "wheel" or "discus" and indicates the shape of the energy points known by that name. Hindu deities are often depicted clasping a serrated one as a formidable weapon of spiritual and physical power. Within each of us, these discs of colored light are spiritual and emotional energy-centers to the physical and etheric bodies, and their condition tells much about their owner's state of emotional, spiritual and even physical well-being, the three frequently being connected. They are in many respects the digestive system of the soul, the part of the constitution that takes sustenance from the cosmos and specific spiritual sources and makes it usable to the individual.

Just as DNA carries the genetic code of physical lineage and the psycho-physical blueprint of the vessel of flesh, the chakras record the subtler patterns of our lives: thoughts, deeds, and all that is emotional or high-level. The soul's chakric structure (aka its astral form) works with the materials available to create the physical body, and (as much as is possible) the circumstances most fitting for the inhabiting soul's next set of lessons and experiences.

As each chakra relates to a separate part of the body, set of glands/hormones, and psycho-spiritual function, it follows that its speed, depth of color, condition, and psychic appendages are indicative. These may be perceived by observation through the third eye or ajna chakra itself, or in whatever other way one receives intuitive information. For example, a cardiac complaint might be visible in the heart chakra as a rift or murky coloring at the center, or the person focusing on it might sense a density of energy. Most likely it will have an emotional and spiritual origin that is also visible to psychic vision. Such manifestations are of course as various as their perceivers and subjects, but, as with the visualizations themselves, certain symbols are universal. A broken heart could manifest as savaged auric fiber or bruised or bloody coloring, while unwillingness to love for fear of rejection may be apparent as an armored area in the chest, or a small, tight box.

We see here the root of psychosomatic illness; emotional problems stored in the aura overlap and infect the relevant part of the physical body. The emotional grievance of a broken heart subsequently disrupts the material health of the body and can bring about a cardiac condition. For those of a sensitive constitution, it is all too easy to literally die of a broken heart—and not just for love; all sorts of anxieties and disappointments may be responsible. Clearly the maintenance of a healthy astral body, chakras included, is of paramount importance to total well-being.

Chakras are also the generators of the aura, the glowing body-sheath of sometimes-visible energy. By maintaining and conditioning them, we influence every aspect of our manifestation and its well-being.

There are seven major chakras in the human body. They are, in descending order: crown, third eye, throat, heart, solar plexus, intestinal, and root. Each relates to a particular gland: pineal, pituitary, thyroid and parathyroid, thymus, pancreas, adrenal, and reproductive, respectively. Each also performs specialized functions, which are indicated below. The Sanskrit name and associated gland are noted in parentheses.

CROWN (SAHASRARA/PINEAL)

The crown chakra is located at the center of the top of the skull. It is a major inlet for prana, the universal life-energy. This is the chakra most relevant to spiritual matters, and its Sanskrit title translates as "thousand-petalled," the lotus of perfection in meditative symbolism. It is an indication of the soul's essential purity that its color is an effulgent white.

THIRD EYE (AJNA/PINEAL/PITUITARY)

Located between and slightly above the eyebrows in the bindi position, this is the center of inner vision, intuition, and innovative ability. The ajna is the third eye of psychic and spiritual insight. Through this chakra we access Akashic information, the contents of the "cosmic library" or universal subconscious. Its color is purple.

THROAT (VISHUDDHA/THYROID)

Connected with communication, spiritual guidance, and the ability to listen (and hear), this is an important "people skills" chakra. It is pertinent to the endocrine and thyroid glands. It is sky-blue or white and located in the middle back of the throat and should ideally be *felt* to vibrate when chanting. Meaning "pure/purification," an emphasis is apparent on speaking and propagating both truth and good will.

Heart (Anahata/Thymus)

This is the green zone in the center of the sternum. Its position allies it to pulmonary as well as cardiac functions. Meaning "unstained," the anahata is the open and innocent part of us all, the essential purity of mind and soul, unbroken by doubt, pain, cynicism and negative emotions. It is strongly associated with the faculty of hope, and is the emotional center regarding love ties, particularly those of an innocent or aspirational nature.

From the heart chakra extend astral/etheric cords that connect the individual karmically and emotionally to relevant people and places, covering many timespans. Consequently, it is possible to use these cords to trace, for example, a soul-bonded partner from a former incarnation, or to employ them as telepathic communication cables.

The properties of this chakra are so extensive, covering literally the entire body, that it becomes clear why the proper functioning of the psychophysical organism requires affection and love, and why the pursuit of it consumes so much of our time on earth.

Solar Plexus (Manipura/Pancreas/Liver)

Located a few inches below the heart chakra, in the soft tissue at the bottom of the rib cage, is the yellow solar plexus chakra. This zone is intimately connected with feelings, emotions, and gut reactions, and is often the real cause of gastrointestinal discomfort and conditions such as IBS in times of nervousness and stress.

Like the heart chakra, the solar plexus is also a center for telepathic and empathetic communication. The cords that extend from it are representative of one's interaction with other entities, their thickness depending on how frequent the contact has been, and the level of its impact.

Unfortunately, these ties bind us just as tightly to people we hate as to people we love, sometimes more so. There is no better way to build up a lasting psychic rapport with someone than to feel strongly about them, either positively or negatively. Conversely, the best way to avoid being bound with another is to block them from your mind and render them irrelevant from the start, though this can be extremely hard to manage when one feels, angry, insulted, rejected, endangered, or any of the plethora of emotions that blight most of us from time to time. There is more to the advice "turn the other cheek" (i.e., fail to react) than straightforward pacifism: hurt feelings blur our judgment and can wreak havoc; allowing oneself the chance to calm down, chant a mantra, and regain perspective before reacting is always wise though all too often impossible. No wonder so many yogis and mystics live alone in forests and caves! If it can be attained, ignorance really is the best form of defense. No unnecessary interaction, no hindrance to one's spiritual ascent. The cords connecting us with people and places of little personal significance are, of course, the thinnest and most difficult to trace.

The manipura center is also connected with morality issues, worldly ambition, and vice.

INTESTINAL *(SVADHISHTHANA/ADRENAL)*

This orange, spinning disc is connected with our faculty of interpretation, as well as with digestive and endocrinal functions. Body fluids are controlled from this zone, as are charisma and vitality levels. It therefore affects our ability and desire to interact with others. The intestinal chakra lies halfway down the stomach, between the navel and genitals.

ROOT *(ROOT/MULADHARA/TESTES OR OVARIES)*

The red base chakra relates to sexuality, connection to earth, and instinctive feelings, such as fear in life-threatening situations. If we have a purely sexual relationship with somebody, they will be connected to us primarily through this chakra (although purely sexual relationships are in fact very rare, being more of a function of incomplexity than our spiritual constitutions will normally allow).

The intestinal and base chakras share the function of sustaining our physical response to sex, though all of the chakras have an influence in one way or another on our proper response to psychosexual stimuli. The immune system and basic survival modes are also controlled by the root energy center.

Chants and Mantras

We are blessed by Hinduism and Buddhism especially with a wealth of ancient, scientific mantras immaculately attuned to each individual deity; indeed,

Sanskrit words and intonations are deemed to be godforms in and of themselves. Thanks to the complimentary wonders of the modern world, these spiritual formulae are now accessible online, along with translations, correct intonation, pronunciation and so on. This is the most incredible asset to the spiritual seeker.

Of course, different strokes for different folks, but the reader is encouraged to access and practice these chants as their intelligence and intuition dictates. To *jaap* (chant reverently) with a *mala* (prayer beads with which to count the repetitions, usually to 108)—or even silently and entirely immobile—is one of the easiest means of shedding ego and gaining spiritual insight. It soon becomes evident that the syllables, sounds and words are indeed living entities and that the deities concerned abide within the mantras and are activated by their repetition.

The neurological as well as spiritual effects of this simple tool are nothing short of mind-blowing, and the reader is encouraged to delve further. For our purposes here, relevant mantras may be found at the end of the initial descriptive passage on each Hindu goddess.

Aum/Om

The Sanskrit word ॐ is often spelled *om* but properly pronounced *aum.* Meditation on it prior to any and all of these exercises will help immensely. This syllable embodies being and not-being; it is ultra-reality in the form of sound. For meditative purposes it is usually intoned "AU" as in "home," higher pitched; "UUU" as in "moon," slightly lower; proceeded by an emphatic "MMMM," lower pitched still. These syllables represent the cosmic processes of creation (Brahma), preservation (Vishnu), and dissolution (Shiva), and contain all that is possible to be created, done, thought, and believed... and arguably plenty more besides! Sanskrit and mantra are mediated by Saraswati, who gives musical and linguistic form to concept.

Sometimes it is preferable to make the "aum" sound aloud, vibrating it from your lower throat upward, with the final part at the front of the mouth. It is good to vibrate it wholly while running it up and down your spine and through your chakras, but this depends on circumstance and levels of privacy: obviously, inhibition does not aid inner tranquility. A good alternative or supplement to chanting out loud is provided by the many excellent recordings of Hindu and Tibetan mantras now widely available. There are some superb samples on YouTube, for example. The dramatic atmospherics can thus be absorbed privately on headphones. The sometimes rather alarming-sounding ceremonies of Tibetan monks especially contain an extremely high dosage of "aum" and are excellent for helping evoke the sound in one's head.

Once you are familiar with mantras, it is possible and often desirable to chant them mentally, whether using a mala, asanas, a musical instrument, or without movement.

Index of Goddess Functions

Purpose	Goddess
Abuse, coping with	Kali
Amends, making	Nephthys
Athletics	Artemis
Attraction	
–of a sexual partner	Aphrodite
–of a long-term partner	Radha and Isis
–of money	Lakshmi
Balance	Ma'at, Iris
Beauty	Aphrodite, Isis
Body shape, changing	Artemis, Sekhmet
Chakras, conditioning	Iris
Change	
–accepting	Persephone
–encouraging	Saraswti
Coming out as gay, trans, or other	Durga, Hecate

Purpose	Goddess
Communication skills	Iris
Complacency/status quo	
–challenging	Kali
–attaining	Hathor, Lakshmi
Confidence	Durga, Kali
Creativity	Saraswati
Depression, combating	Persephone, Saraswati
Desire	Aphrodite
Diplomacy	Iris
Discrimination, combating	Hecate, Ma'at
Divination	Isis
Endurance	Hathor, Artemis
Exam performance	Saraswati
Exorcising the past	Kali, Persephone, Radha
Faithfulness	Isis
Fertility	Hathor, Isis, Lakshmi
Friendship, creating against the odds	Hecate
Gender fluidity	Artemis
Getting even	Durga, Hecate, Kali, Ma'at
Growth	Hathor
Happiness	Lakshmi
Healing	Isis, Nephthys, Saraswati
Inspiration	Saraswati, Isis

Purpose	Goddess
Integration	Hecate, Iris
Intuition	Isis
Justice	Hecate, Ma'at, Iris
Love	
–attaining long-term	Isis
–attaining sexual	Aphrodite
–letting go temporarily	Radha
–letting go permanently	Radha
Magickal ability	Isis
Money	Lakshmi
Nurturing	Hathor
Phobias, overcoming	Kali
Physical fitness	Artemis
Prejudice, overcoming	Hecate
Psychism	Hecate, Isis
Separation	
–coping with or causing	Radha
Sexuality	Aphrodite
Shamanism	Sekhmet
Shape-shifting	Sekhmet, Artemis, Isis
Strength	
–emotional	Durga, Kali
–physical	Artemis
Stuck in the mud; escaping	Saraswati

Purpose	Goddess
Study	Saraswati
Success	Lakshmi
Truth	Ma'at
Weight gain/loss	Artemis
Wisdom	Hecate, Ma'at, Saraswati
Witchcraft skills	Hecate, Isis, Persephone, Sekhmet

PART I
HINDU
GODDESSES

CHAPTER 1

SARASWATI

Usually she can be found by the sacred river's edge, or floating on her lotus, her black hair flowing down a moon-white sari, the air alive with the mellifluous music of her vina. Saraswati's fingers on the strings cause golden ages to arise, and when she ceases from her craft, civilizations fall and the universe is diminished.

She sits in mantric meditation, a crescent moon upon her forehead, bindi of light, drawing deities from her potent spoken spells.

She crafts the notes into yantras, geometric shapes infused with Vedic energy. These she may give as rewards to her favorite poets, sages, and winsome minstrels wandering lost in the world of delusion, of Maya.

She will dip her admirers in the river of despair, blacker even than her pure black hair, or make them dance spinning into the mire; then on Hamsa, the pure white swan of infinite transcendence, she will glide to them, offering gifts.

A searing draft of inspiration to unclog the blocked channel; a suddenly discovered talent to the sensitive whose skills seemed useless; an iron will unto the genius whose mind kept slipping sideways, downward into matter, undisciplined. Thus will she hone her devotees to perfection once they have been baptized in her eternal waters.

Silver as moonlight she glides, a breath of fragrant hope floating above the tumultuous depths of ignorance; her gifts of speech, culture, and religious quest the rafts of our religious transiting.

Look! Beyond the river sits a gleaming city of many marvels— Saraswati's citadel of astral gold, as yet uninhabited. A populace big enough to fill it must first brave the treacherous waters, following the Muse—and utopia will be theirs.

In the meantime, bards may sing and others dream of her promise, elevating thought and art, with every aspiration moving one step closer to fulfilment of Saraswati's gifts, and of the soul's sublime potential.

Aum Hrim Aim Kreem Saraswati Deviya Namaha

SARASWATI IS ONE OF the *Tridevi*, or holy trinity of goddesses in Hinduism, along with Lakshmi and Parvati. She is Goddess of Supreme Wisdom, Knowledge, Language, and the Arts. In some scriptures she appears as a female counterpart or *Shakti* of Vishnu, along with his wife Lakshmi. In other versions she is wife of Brahma, God of Creation, sometimes his daughter, and occasionally both. According to the *Matsya Purana*, for example, Brahma creates Saraswati as he meditates upon pure goodness, doing this in different descriptions from his mouth, navel, or seminal fluid. The new goddess is so effulgently beautiful that he soon falls in love with her. Anxious to escape his amorous advances, the modest Saraswati positions herself out of his direct gaze. In order to view his creation, Brahma creates another face. Saraswati moves, and again Brahma generates new features with which to appreciate his daughter, eventually totalling five. At this point Saraswati flees to Shiva for protection; he promptly sobers Brahma by tearing off his topmost, or fifth, head—representative of ego. Contrite, Brahma resolves to bless his daughter instead of pursuing her, giving her the free-flowing assets of a river with the ability to irrigate the minds and souls of men; bestowing her with the ability to gift speech to mankind; and finally, having her reside within his very form, so that he might never stultify and always learn more.

At times Saraswati is paired with Ganesha or with a local god pertaining to the arts. Considering the great antiquity of Hinduism—its primary dissemination by *shruti,* or spoken word—and its spread over a vast continent as well as to other countries, disparities are not surprising. However, she is usually depicted alone, happily independent, belonging to no individual, just as the arts themselves belong not to their creator so much as to humanity itself.

Saraswati's name means "fluid" or "flowing," as is water that can be river or lake or rain; as is a spirit when joyful to be part of the universe, imaginative and inspired; as is good music, poetry, inspiration itself. She is also known as *Vak,* or speech: Saraswati offers the tools by which to reflect upon and thus understand one's human nature, and its ultimate truth—all is connected and we are without exception each part of the Absolute. Thus her name also means "one who bestows essence of self." In her aspects of Supreme Goddess of Speech, *Vagisvari* (she is sometimes said to derive from the five tongues of Brahma) and of Wisdom, *Mahavidya,* Saraswati is seen as the mother of the *Rig-Veda;* all of the scriptures are her metaphorical children. She also features in the Puranas as Goddess of Language and Linguistics, often foiling demonic entities through this medium. For example, at the request of the devas for help against the demon Kumbhakarna, Saraswati cunningly twists his tongue as he claims a divine boon, thus causing him to request "Nidra-Asan," or sleep, rather than "Indra-Asan," or the seat of Indra. When the god-hating demon Rakshasa has undergone austerities and is

Saraswati

about to claim a boon from Brahma, Saraswati again steps in and causes him to say, instead of "nirdevanta"—let there be no gods—the subtly different-sounding "nirdratva," or "let me sleep." He promptly falls into a slumber from which he can awake only once every six months. Thus, Saraswati is a goddess of precision in execution, of absolute clarity. Her tricks demonstrate the dire consequences of speaking carelessly, and the spell-like properties latent in each syllable, each seed-sound.

Presiding over language and its articulation, Saraswati is also matron goddess of theater and thaumaturgy; of enlightenment through entertainment. Playwrights, actors, and all involved with the arts appeal to Sarawati for divine inspiration. The knowledge and skill she provides are yogic—that is, they unite body and spirit, opening the psychic constitution to be filled by the waters of the Divine. This in turn channels spiritual bliss and potential liberation. In contrast, many of the arts associated with Lakshmi are commercial, pleasurably time-wasting, and are subsequently deemed impure from a Brahmic standpoint, although Lakshmi when worshipped in her entirety also offers wisdom and morality. However, it is Saraswati who denotes *moksha-patni*, the arts that generate liberating wisdom. This in turn leads to skill and all sorts of self-development that can help harness wealth, symbolized by Lakshmi: although popularly depicted as rivals or antitheses, Saraswati and Lakshmi can in fact bring highly complementary elements.

In the *Rig-Veda* particularly, the oldest of the Hindu scriptures, Saraswati features as a river goddess, thus denoting fertility, free-flowing spirituality, and the purity and life-giving properties of water. Later on her fertility came to be regarded as primarily cerebral rather than physical; she is the spring of inspiration, imagination, and creativity, as well as of language and learning. In the *Rig-Veda*, the river Saraswati runs a now-arid course parallel to the ancient Indus, from the Himalayas northwestward to the sea. The present-day river associated with her, the Sarsuti, runs a quite different course: the "drying up of the Saraswati river," on whose banks the Vedas themselves were most likely written, could either be taken literally, or as a metaphor regarding the drought of spiritual wisdom of this era, the Kali Yuga. Debate continues as to the exact location of the river this goddess once personified; aerial photographs have recently been revealed of what some scholars deem to be its original course before India's territory was divided as it is now; opposition to this theory is inevitably political as much as scriptural.

Whatever the case regarding her geographic embodiment, the now-independent Saraswati's connection with initiations and religious experiences is clear, as is her affiliation with all water, or spirit, which flows to earth from the heavens, and with the concomitant hydraulics, which require intelligent study to apply and which are symbolic of all fruitful endeavor. In the Vedas, India is sometimes referred to as *Sapta Sindhu,* land of seven rivers; of these, it is the Indus river which later gave the word *Hindu* via the Greeks to the populace of its latter-day banks, and the word *India* to Bharat.

As well as acting as a territorial border, the crossing of a river denotes the oft-troublesome transit from old circumstances to new, and bathing of course represents rebirth; as such Saraswati also presides over healing properties and processes. She is a baptism-epiphany goddess, and guards over the processes thus engendered.

Saraswati is also a source and upholder of emotions such as nostalgia, hope and inspiration—essential ingredients of any musician, bard or artist. She is the Muse herself: music, poetry, and scholarly success are amongst the boons she can bring. She improves memory, and is approached for aid in study and educational issues. Chanting her mantras can improve learning skills and fend off mental deterioration and senility. She is widely worshipped in India as Goddess of Culture and Learning, her spiritual presence in schools and universities being equally vital to that of the teachers, books and pens— and nowadays, computers—that are venerated in conjunction with her. Her associations with sound and meaning make the singing or chanting of mantras an especially beneficial manner in which to approach Saraswati.

Saraswati represents the essence and meaning of the Vedas; thus all knowledge, sacred and secular, originates from her. Naturally she is honored as mother of Sanskrit, most ancient, holiest and wholly spiritually precise of languages. Riding Brahma's white swan, Hamsa, she glides above the murky imperfections of the material (earth) plane, the graceful epitome of purity, intelligence and transcendence. She is divine eloquence. The creation of all the worlds and their inhabitants is accredited to Saraswati and Brahma during their celestial honeymoon, a singing into being of multiple thoughtforms through sheer joy and playfulness, which, like Lakshmi's lovemaking with Vishnu, lasted many ages.

Saraswati is also *Mataji*, the divine mother of her devotees, the homely and nurturing aspect of copious Hindu goddesses. Even the ferocious Kali is often approached as such, and will indeed respond favorably to the trust her "children" necessarily invest in her. However, where Kali represents necessary destruction and dissolution, Saraswati, rarely fierce and ever-dreamy, preferring the power of the word over that of the sword, personifies creative intelligence. As such she is represented as dazzlingly white, clad in a moon-bright sari—a luminary in the world of dark ignorance. Because she is instigator of the arts, she is matchless in grace and beauty, an expert in the endless variations of the celestial dance. Her name reflects the lucid, luminous, liquid qualities of her form and movements.

When depicted, Saraswati sometimes has one face and four hands; sometimes five faces, eight hands, and three eyes; and on occasion, in her *Mahasaraswati* aspect of Durga/Parvati, she also sports a blue neck. Her first four hands hold a *vina* (lute), *aksamala* (rosary), *padma* (lotus flower), and *pushtaka* (book). The other four clutch a *sankha* (conch shell), *chakra* (discus), *trishula* (trident), and *ankusa* (elephant goad). The rosary is illustrative of spiritual sciences: yoga, meditation and mantras. In Saraswati's case it is often made of pearls, white as Indian moonlight in autumn, one of her seasonal attributions; sometimes this is substituted with a crystal *mala*: another type of beaded prayer-chain or "garland". The discus shows that she is not without defence: a chakra properly thrown is a formidable weapon, and the same may of course be said of the trident. The chakra also incorporates into Saraswati's repertoire of human excellence the dimension of physicality and athletics. She is a balanced goddess, quick to indicate the proper and timely use of our skills to further human development—hence also the elephant goad, provoking this symbol of heavy, dense matter swiftly in a specific direction, overruling it with intelligence. Lord Ganesha uses the same tool to remove obstacles from the path of Dharma. Worshipped in schools and universities, the attribution to Saraswati of these tools of self-improvement makes perfect sense.

The lotus flower represents the unfolding of all life in perfection, and its microcosm, the individual crown chakra; while the lute demonstrates creative rendition. Conch shells represent alertness and the act of listening, as well as having obvious aquatic associations. Saraswati's noose suggests that we may hang ourselves by overindulgence in one area or talent; that life is finite so no time to waste, and suggests the self-eliminating impulse experienced by many creative and spiritual types who find themselves helplessly mired in the maya-matrix: the mundane, illusory world. Overcoming the challenges of the Dark Night of the Creative Soul is itself an initiation.

The peacocks by which Saraswati is often accompanied are beloved of the Hindu pantheons and particularly sacred to Krishna, gentle god of love and attraction; they carry a double meaning. In one sense peacocks are regal and beautiful, their plumage apparently featuring the all-seeing eye; they symbolize the full glory of spiritual practice and the opening of the ajna and crown chakras particularly. In another, they have long been associated with ostentation and the dangers of the material world, primarily of pride, and their piercing screech and unattractive feet have upheld this dichotomy. However, the self-aggrandizement and ignorance that they can symbolize would of course be held well in check by a divine entity, so they keep their tails closed in the company of Saraswati, aware of the wisdom of humility. We should not "display" our knowledge for its own sake, or in order to outshine others. Their beauty is intense, however, as a reflection of the divine: "The Pride of the Peacock is the Glory of God," as poet-artist William Blake put it in *Proverbs of Hell*.

Saraswati is often depicted with a swan, representing the ability to glide over the murky waters of imperfection; or with a goose, a bird reputedly able to separate milk from water, or spiritual truth from falsehood.

Thus Saraswati is the civilizer, the impulse to evolve, taking humanity step-by-step from cave to computer, from clodhopping to Bharatanatyam (Indian classical dance), from flesh-tearing brutality to intelligent discernment and finest cuisine (again aligning her with Lakshmi, generally deemed a more materialistic deity: but both are needed). She would rebuke, however, any insular extreme—hence one of her symbols being the noose—expressiveness and unity of mind, body and spirit are paramount to her criteria, just as in any good school's curriculum: mindfulness, meditation and respect for the sacred should be taught along with the sciences, humanities and arts.

All that unites profound thought and learning with spiritual intuition and creativity, lies in her domain.

Approaching Saraswati: Preparation

Saraswati presides over evening prayer, and early evening is an appropriate time to approach her; the fuller the moon the better, as Saraswati is said to "shine like many moons" herself. She is sometimes described as being smeared in sandalwood paste, so sandalwood incense is beneficial in evoking her.

Saraswati's *puja* is celebrated in early spring, thus buds and spring flowers, especially yellow ones, will also help to create the environment conducive to this goddess. A bath with lotus or ylang-ylang oil should help you relax and get you on the right wavelength. Light candles of white and yellow, and contemplate the perfection and unsullied beauty you are about to encounter; listen to some relaxing music as you prepare (preferably mantras, kirtan, sitar…). Appreciate the skill, both spiritual and practical, that went into its composition. One would be nothing without the other—we all know of music that is emotional drivel, or conversely, empty melodic structures; this balance is one of Saraswati's major facets. In her, the practical is elevated by higher feeling, and high-flying ideals are earthed through skill and craftsmanship. She is the force that brings the strands of interlacing harmony to the mind of the musician, who listens and writes, or plays them spontaneously. She is the music of the spheres, an audible sacred geometry. Consider how poetry, sculpture, and innovative art spring up whenever she is near.

Meditation on AUM is the ideal start to these exercises.

When you have relaxed, surrounded yourself with pleasant scents, and performed your preparations, meditate on the "aum" sound for as long as it takes to get fully in the mood.

You are now ready to encounter Saraswati on the inner planes.

Exercise for Inspiration

Sit comfortably on your floor, chair or bed, keeping your spine as straight as possible. If you are a yogi/yogini in training (or actual) and can manage lotus posture or some other suitable asana, all the better.

Having laid the mantric foundation with the "aum" sound, you are ready to progress to recital of one of the simplest and best mantras for balanced creative pursuits: that of "aum kring kring kring." Strictly speaking, this should be chanted (or mouthed while mentally chanting) at least 108 times, counted out on a rosary/mala. Completing the mantra will guarantee your success, so it is well worth setting aside the time to see it through. It will also create a mood conducive to the following visualization.

Start all the exercises by assuming the posture most comfortable to you but which won't induce sleep, and draw a few deep breaths. Golden light is pouring into the top of your head. Be aware of your chakras, starting at the tailbone and rising up; of your state as spirit made manifest. Gradually, the chakras begin to turn and whir, and as the speed increases, so does the light flowing into and from them; at first slowly, dimly, like a lamp in fog; then brighter, sharper, more effusively. Continue this process until the light-producing motion is firmly established in your mind's eye, your body is shining with colour, and preferably, until you can physically feel the glow.

Now, mentally link the pulsating, growing energy of your tailbone area with the zone above and between your eyes.

Breathe in deeply and out deeply, aware of the base chakra's light beginning to seep upward as you do so.

Next, deliberately and firmly pull this red energy up your spine toward your third eye area. Notice how the two types of chakra-energy combine to form a deep reddish-indigo. Your base chakra continues to spin brightly, infused with the purple color from your third eye zone. Now your base chakra, spine, and pineal gland are all glowing with a vibrant indigo-red.

Holding this color strongly in your mind's eye, take a deep breath of light and imagine you are traveling in lotus posture over a vast purple sea whose waves shimmer in a thousand hues of purple and red, creating sharp and subtle colors you would never have thought possible, so subtle, diaphanous and multidimensional are they.

The sky in which you are levitating is also purple, but a deeper, more intense shade punctuated from time to time by passing distant moons—silvery-white orbs whose light seems to make you travel faster and higher. You can change speed and direction with a flick of the switch of will, but at

Saraswati

the moment you are happy to be traveling through such a beautiful astral space on your way to supplicate the great goddess Saraswati.

After a while you begin to perceive thin silver cords around you, invisible to your outer vision, but you can feel them growing thicker; reminiscent of the strings of a lute. They seem, on closer inspection, to be vibrating with infinitely pure atoms of skilfully plucked sound. There are many of them being sounded at once, and you are traveling faster still into the heart of this symphony, your vision sharp and senses rejoicing in this astral wonder.

Now, call to Saraswati.

Ask her to allow you to approach her in search of inspiration.

All around you are tiny atoms of pranic energy, vibrating very quickly and making you envision each as a universe in its own right. Your body is also charged with positive energy: the prana is permeating you even as you hang suspended in Saraswati's sacred space.

Before you know it, a glowing white figure sitting serenely in a lotus flower is gliding toward you. You can see the tiny red light of her bindi from here, like a rose petal on snow. Gracefully you begin to fly toward her, still in lotus posture. Even as you think it you arrive, touching her feet in humility.

Saraswati's hand alights on your crown chakra, sending vivid shots of energy into your brain and down your spinal cord. The purple sky, which you know is saturated with all the energy of all the universes, is being absorbed into your body via the top of your head, your ears, your mouth, and through the back of your neck, at the medulla oblongata.

Observe Saraswati, Goddess of all the Arts; and how she interacts with you. When you feel fully charged with creative ability and potential, thank her.

Wait for Saraswati to depart before you do. Never turn your back on her—social graces are important to this goddess—the same of course goes for all deities. Politeness will be rewarded, while rudeness and laziness are anathema to Saraswati, most cultivated and courteous of goddesses.

Observe everything you experience as she leaves and as you return, and when you do, open your eyes and immortalize the experience as a thank-you offering to Saraswati—write it as a story or poem; paint it; turn it into music or dance. Such a gift cannot fail to please the Mistress of the Arts.

Visualization for Self-Healing:
Aiding Transition and Change

Saraswati can also be approached for healing powers, for yourself and others, especially if the ailment is psychological and connected with trauma or maladjustment to change. Depression after a bereavement or agoraphobia as a result of an unwelcome move or loss of social status are examples of Saraswati's potential healing domain. She helps us transcend our concerns and take a fatalistic overview—in its most positive sense. An advanced Hindu neither celebrates good nor bemoans loss, and is aware that circumstances on this plane are continually in flux and that pleasures and pains are merely transitory; in some respects, Saraswati embodies this belief. However, through Saraswati the intense experiences are not simply endured, but are sublimated into the arts; thus even the destructive becomes creative.

A visualization along this vein could bring you the necessary zest and courage to break out of a low period and try something creative and new; anything from learning a new language to writing a song or a poem. Saraswati teaches us that everything happens for a positive purpose, and she can help us cross that difficult river of change, be cleansed, and reach the shore in safety.

Sit quietly, shut your eyes, and mentally gather together all of your negative feelings about the situation you have been undergoing. Think of the things you would like to leave behind—those aspects of your life that have been hindering your progress. Bundle all of your hurt, disappointment, and reticence into a big black bag; take as long as you need to strongly feel and envision this process.

Now, visualize yourself standing at a river's edge. This side of the bank represents your past, the river is the process of change, and on the other side awaits your new, liberated life.

Take the big black bag of woes and bury it by the water's edge. Again, take as long as you need to properly complete this task.

Feeling relieved, if a little rootless, you resolve to cross the river to inhabit your new life. In you wade until you are waist-deep in water. Behind you is everything that has become obsolete in your life, and all of the negative feelings about the situation you have been enduring.

Saraswati

Notice how the ground feels beneath your feet: rocky, slippery, sandy. The water itself represents your present state of being, and it may be murky, clear, fast-moving, tranquil, or turmoiled; your inner eye will tell you how it is. Either way, you know that the stretch of river before you is very deep and that you are likely to have difficulty sustaining your direction. Can you make it to the other side?

For a moment or two, contemplate how you are going to cross. Think of all the good things waiting for you over there—your creature comforts, empathetic company, exciting new experiences. Try to feel enthusiasm for this future, even if only because it has to be better than your present situation. You will need to employ all of your willpower to help you across. Determine not to be washed downstream or deflected from your course.

You cast your inner eye around for something to help you reach the opposite bank. It looks quite inviting now, but there is a danger of being swept away if you forge any farther ahead.

Suddenly, you see a huge, brilliant swan floating down the river toward you. On its back is a woman in white robes, resplendent and smiling. Your main impression of her is a mass of flowing, fragrant, mellifluous light that is intelligent, compassionate, and divine. As she glides toward you, try to mentally connect with her and ask for her boons.

Explain to Saraswati why you are stuck. Describe the problem that initiated your depression or stultification, and emphasize that you are eager to reach the other side of the river and the new life that waits for you there. Take as long as you need for this prayer-like supplication.

When you emerge from your inner monologue, you find that a large lotus leaf is floating beside the white bird. With a swish of her slender hand, Saraswati invites you to climb onto the leaf. She tells you to concentrate on reaching the other side of the river. As you focus, you start to move.

You are aware that Saraswati is behind you, ready to help if any trouble occurs.

As you draw closer to the riverbank you notice a small temple with the aum sign painted on it, red against yellow. There is wonderful, strange music coming out of the temple, and its unusual architecture fascinates you. Its stained glass windows are amazingly crafted and intense, inspiring colors beam from the building.

When you reach the other side of the river, dismount and step with assurance onto the new terrain. You turn to thank the goddess, but she is gone.

Excited by the adventure and eager to explore this new land so full of beautiful intriguing things, you head for the temple in order to thank Saraswati.

No sooner have you thought it than your feet rise off the ground and you are delivered to the threshold, where a potent wave of billowing incense and vibrant sound engulfs you. Feel the Aum running up and down your spine, through your limbs, jiggling every atom of your body. In the smoky sound flash all kinds of colors; subtle and vivid shades, pulsating violet hues, and streaks of red and flowing blue.

If you are wearing astral shoes at this point, kick them off before crossing the temple threshold.

As you enter, you feel as if your body is being shaken by incredible mechanical thunder but welcome it, as you know it is breaking up the clay straitjacket of your previous monotonous existence and exposing the brighter subtle body beneath it.

Soon, you are feeling very light and agile and are impatient to explore this new land in your new vehicle. Find the shrine and pluck a candle, a string of flowers, or a cake from the ether; place it at the foot of the altar and thank Saraswati for guiding you into the next cycle of your incarnation.

Now, leave the temple and come back to your body. Remember that you are anxious to get out and experience all the wonderful things this new land has to offer. You will deliberately seek the unusual.

Open your eyes, and when you are ready, write down everything you have experienced in this visualization. Analyze it if you so desire: what or who did you see when you were looking for help to reach the other side? Does the water seem calmer to you now in retrospect? What were you standing on before you were rescued? Perhaps you will even start a dream-diary now—why not? The subconscious is a fascinating thing, after all; who's to say that one reality is any more substantial or significant than another?

Academic Excellence: Preparation

Saraswati is the ideal deity to whom to appeal in the cause of academe. You may please her simply by appealing to her in a creative manner. Saraswati loathes sterile learning, but logical effort combined with passion and inspiration will gain her favor. The practical and the spiritual must combine. This is a cause particularly fitting to India itself, a country whose spirituality reputedly outweighs its utilitarianism. This imbalance was exploited in the time of the Raj, when India was invaded by those of the opposite makeup. As Jodh Singh ruminates in *The Wild Sweet Witch*, "It is true that we are impractical, visionaries, dreamers … it is because we put the spirit first and these Europeans always think of the material. This is why they are our masters, but the things of the spirit are more important, and there, they are children" (Mason, 88). Happily, Westerners are no longer in any way "masters" of India and its people, but we remain spiritual toddlers in comparison to even the most humble yogis of their number. In Saraswati we find the balance between these extremes of materialism and spirituality; a combination of the best features of each element.

The following meditation is simple, and is best performed in the morning before school, work, or on the day of examination. Lavender, tea tree, eucalyptus, or peppermint oil are excellent evaporated in the room or used in the bath prior to this exercise. They provide a mental tonic and are ideal when concentration is required.

Visualization for Academic Excellence

Sitting comfortably, imagine yourself inside a giant purple egg. This egg is Akasha, the symbol of all knowledge, the source of all understanding and revelation.

Chant mentally or actually the mantra "Aum Aim Kring Saum Saraswatiye Namaha" as many times as you need to get into the zone, 108 being the usual number for a successful Hindu mantra. As you sit there, feel the sharpness of your intellect, your keen desire to learn, and the spiritual presence of Saraswati, who presides over all educational matters.

Admire the deep, unusual purple that fills the air around you: in it abides every atom of creative intelligence ever extant, from the source of primitive building tools to the inspiration of Mozart. This is the origin of every theory on life, death, and the universe; every terrestrial and spiritual achievement.

Nearby, shelves heave with the weight of many books. A faint smell of incense hangs in the air; a hint of an arcane ritual that makes you contemplate the esoteric contents of the tomes. Underlying this is the scent of the books themselves; the pervasive library-smell of aging pages.

Feel yourself being elevated by visiting this sacred space.

Breathe in deeply, and concentrate on your crown and pineal chakras; connect yourself with this incredible pool of illumination.

When you breathe out, imagine the channels of your perception being cleared, creating an information superhighway of your mind.

Continue to breathe consciously in and out until the relationship between you and the Akashic information is firmly established and unquestionable.

Now, imagine your aura fired in purple, like a flame. You are becoming a luminary.

Your resolve is strengthened; you *know* your capacity to be infinite. You can absorb wisdom and inspiration through your crown chakra and third eye at will; the potential is limitless. Abide in this state for as long as you feel is of benefit, or as long as it takes to really believe this cosmic truth.

Return to the room braced and alert, and apply yourself methodically to your study or the matter in hand. This, combined with your awareness of higher things and a clever originality, cannot fail to aid you in the realms of creative academe.

Saraswati

CHAPTER 2

DURGA

Durga the demon-slayer fights clad in her glad rags, her elegance hypnotic and her frailty beguiling.

Mountains of purple rise up behind her, capped by sacred snows and haunted by yogis whose thoughts reach her easily in this pristine atmosphere.

Pockets of ethereal perfume float from the folds of her sari, enticing the senses of the next eager lover. Delicately, she destroys.

As ripe and mellow as a harvest moon she seems, her ten arms poised as if to cut and gather her own crop of bright blessings and hand it to her opponent in surrender; a cunning trick!

Suitors wait in line to challenge her in battle; what better salve to the injured male pride than the taming of this celestial shrew? A million men have lent their virility to Durga, gem of femininity; their admiration only makes her independence stronger.

See how she digs those elegant fingers into her war steed's luxuriant ruff of soft fur! At her bidding, smooth and subtle as a snake's, he carries Durga to some favored vantage point, watched by the envious eyes of her opponents. The beast's pleasured purrings torment them with longing, but his mistress's martial arts keep them ever at bay.

Rather death in the propeller-blades of her arms than this humiliating demise-by-desire!

So they come, one by one, to be unmanned by the skillful swoop of a tender blade-taloned hand, and behind the mirage that is Durga, behold the victorious smile of her kindred spirit, Kali.

With their dying breath they must admit that they misjudged her strength, her nature, and her source.

Durga throws back her beautiful head and laughs. At the sound of her ambrosial merriment, a hundred more step forward for the challenge.

Thus she appears to the enemies of peace, and thus they are conquered.

Aum Dum Durgayei Namaha

DURGA IS PACIFYING AND beautiful, but a formidable enemy. Her name means variously "impenetrable," "distant," and "fortress," though this great goddess is known by many others, spanning as she does a vast array of qualities. In some versions, Durga is self-generated; this best befits her inviolate nature. In others she is created from rays of concentrated thought when the male gods Brahma, Vishnu, and Shiva could do nothing to combat Mahishasura, the great demon. These rays—crimson, white, and lustrous black— danced together in the air, merging and forming a pillar of blinding radiance.

Chapter 2

From this almighty column stepped a being of unsurpassed beauty sitting on a lion: the impenetrable *Shakti,* or divine feminine, epitome of strength, knowledge and spiritual integrity.

Joyfully, the gods lent Devi, as she was then simply known, the sum of their strength and full use of their celestial weapons. In iconography she is depicted with up to twenty arms, indicating her speed, dexterity, and intelligence, each hand holding a different symbol. Most often she carries a sharp sword, serrated-edged discus, a golden bell (with which to confuse the demons), a wine cup and water pot for sustenance and flow on the battlefield, a bow, infallible arrows, and Shiva's terrifying trident. A dart, iron rod and axe are amongst the other weapons frequently attributed to her.

Depicting the gentler side of her nature, Durga also bears forth the lotus flower of peace, representing the eternal, blissful abode of spirit and its many aspects; a rosary for meditation and mantra; a shield, and a conch with which to call forth her fellow warriors against injustice. Often she clasps one of Indra's lightning bolts, an intimidating scepter, and other symbols of her insuperable power, tools blessed by the other gods to render her unconquerable. She is clad in a red sari, the color of blood. She is often depicted accompanied by the monkey god Hanuman, who in the *Durga Chalisa* (devotional hymns to Durga) is said to fight with her. Like Kali, Durga is consort of Shiva, of whom Hanuman is occasionally said to be another form, here embodying the four yogas (*bhakti, raja, jnana,* and *karma yoga*). Hanuman is the perfect devotee of the gods and battles with them against injustice. Durga's mount—variously a lion or tiger, or an elephant-tiger hybrid—shows her control over dharma, her courage, and of course adds to her speed, ferocity, and agility.

As with all Hindu lineages, due to their great antiquity and the significant geographical and linguistic variants involved, facts about Durga vary. Hinduism is richer with myths depicting the gods than any other culture or religion, and each locale may have its own versions and nomenclature. There are thus numerous godforms to whom to pay select devotions; one for every specific requirement. What is consistent in all versions of Durga however is her great righteous ferocity, bravery, and will to maintain cosmic balance.

Known by 108 primary names, Durgadevi's versatility is beyond doubt. In the *Ramayana,* she is sent into mortal combat with the world-threatening

Danavasic Asura (demonic demi-god) Durg. After a gory victory, the goddess adopts the name Durga, indicative of her frightful powers, her ability to consume the enemy and thus take on their strength and positive attributes. She is also called *Parvati* (aligning her again with Kali as consort of Shiva), *Kaarali* (the violent), *Varada* (Granter of Boons), *Papaharini* (Destroyer of Sin), *Arogyada* (She Who Grants Good Health), and numerous other appellations. As *Trinetra*, her third eye is referenced: like Shiva, she has an actual eye between her brows. Each name indicates a particular trait or quality the supplicant wishes to appeal to or worship. *Karalika,* for example, tears enemies to shreds, while as *Bhaavini,* the same goddess is simply overwhelming in her beauty. Hindu brides and wives appeal to Durga for the numerous qualities required for a successful marriage.

Primarily, Durga is known for facing the formidable buffalo-demon Mahishasura, who has cunningly performed many penances and hardships—*tapasyas*—in order to elicit a boon from Lord Brahma. Because he thought all women beneath contempt, the demon's wish was merely that no god, man, or animal should ever be able to kill him. Following the granting of this boon, Mahishasura considered himself invincible and thus went on to wreak bloody, universal havoc, eventually bringing the worlds to their knees. In desperation, the gods convened to deduce a means of annihilating this rampant demon. Realizing that the Asura had arrogantly excluded women from his list of potential foes, they created the great warrior-goddess Durga to track and slay him. In somewhat preferable versions, Durgadevi is invoked rather than created by the male deities; however, the former genesis is the most commonly cited.

Either way, Mahishasura hears of Durga's incredible beauty, and wishes to meet and marry her. She laughingly responds that she will marry only the one who can defeat her in battle. The arrogant Mahishasura eagerly accepts her challenge.

In some versions, Durga charges straight into battle, her various forms and warriors taking on Mahishasura's demons while she tackles the giant Asura himself. In others, she begins by lulling him into a false sense of security by playing divine music on her flute or a vina, causing him to become even more overwhelmed by her effulgent beauty. In all cases, the attack culminates with the divine Durga crushing the head of Mahishasura beneath her foot. The delusion of feminine frailty wins her the battle, along with her subtle and perfectly honed martial ability, limitless stamina in the cause of peace, and tactical skill.

When angry, Durga is closely associated with Kali; indeed, Kali is sometimes manifested as an embodiment of Durga's fury, or even birthed from Durga's third eye: and they have fought side by side against many demons—always, of course, emerging victorious. The most important aspects of Durga in the context of this book, however, are her personal strength and independence. She uses her "male" power to fulfil her own ends and is never personally compromised. One translation of her name is "Unapproachable One," referring in part to her physical location—normally, isolated mountainous regions; it also refers to her refusal to interact personally with her suitors or supplicants ... unless she is slaying them, of course.

Durga has nine main forms, and as such is known as Navadurga. Her most popular festivals or pujas punctuate March and October and are known respectively as Chaitra Navaratri and Sharad Navaratri, the latter word translating as nine nights of worship. During each of the consecutive twenty-four hours, Durga is worshipped and propitiated with fasting; chanting of mantras; offerings of flowers, incense, and light; and individual prayers to each of her aspects.

Again, practices vary according to region, and Navaratri incorporates the praising of Lakshmi and Saraswati. Together Durga, Lakshmi, and Saraswati are Tridevi, the triple Shakti. Generally however Durga Puja involves welcoming the goddess as back to her home; dressing her statues richly and making offerings to her; rituals in which her battles are vividly recalled and her female devotees ululate as if at her side in battle; celebrating the goddess victorious; accepting her as a literal harvest of food, hence her connection with the harvest festival; and on the final day, bidding her farewell as she returns to her distant abode in Mount Kailash. On this last day, married women smear the statues of Durga, themselves and one another with the vermilion paste sindoor in order to elicit a happy marriage, and the clay statues of the goddess are paraded to the water and immersed so that they will dissolve.

Durga's nine major aspects demonstrate her versatility and omnipotence. On each day of Durga Puja, a different facet of the great Devi is lauded. She is sometimes wild: in this aspect Durga is worshipped on the first day of the Festival as the daughter of the Himalayas, as Nature and as wife of Shiva. In this form, usually called Shailaputri, she rides the celestial white bull, Nandi. Here she is deemed to be an incarnation of Sati, Shiva's renunciant wife who in meditation reduced herself to a skeleton and eventually immolated herself in protest and shame when her own father insulted her husband. As Shailaputri, the goddess is the wilderness itself, as well as the blissful asceticism and perfect harmony that is achieved by living in such a primal and pure environment, free from earthly pride, greed and competition. This is the ego-free state to which all good Hindu ascetics aspire. She is also Parvati, and the goddess corresponding to the Muladhara or root chakra, and to the Moon. Yogis will meditate on raising their kundalini energy from this point throughout Navaratri.

Secondly, Durga manifests as Brahmacharini: in this nun-like form she carries only prayer beads (a mala) and water pot (a kamandal), and again the emphasis is on piety, austerity, and the simplicity of communion with divinity as the most essential facet of soul and psyche (to put it in modern terms). She follows God alone.

Durga's third form is that of the righteously furious Chandraghanta, in which she emanates golden light and on her radiant brow bears a half moon, symbolic also of Shiva. She rides a magnificent lion and holds her weapons aloft in ten hands, the very epitome of the just warrior goddess, and corresponds with planet Mars. The ringing of bells is of particular significance to this avatar, as the vibrations from her ghanta (bell) are said to have eradicated many of her foes. The significance of sound in Hinduism supersedes that even of light in other creeds; all and everything comes down to seed-sounds, the sacred Aum.

As a happy creatrix, actually having fun as she presides over the worlds, Durga manifests as the solar Kushmanda, creating this universe in the form of the Akashic egg and birthing it from sun through her blissfully humorous smile. It is good to be reminded that this goddess knows how to enjoy herself and is at play as well as in meditation and at war in her numerous avatars.

Durga (/Parvati) is said to have given birth to Skanda, warrior son of Shiva, and as such she is known as Skanda Mata. This prodigious offspring is chief commander of the celestial Devic forces as they battle against the infernal Danavasic Asuras. He par-originates from Murugan, whose mount is a peacock. On the fifth day of Durga Puja she is thus worshipped as mother, small child in her lap, serene protectress and giver of physical health.

Next comes the day devoted to a wisdom-aspect of Durga in which she is praised as Katyayani, daughter of the sage Katyayan. Riding a lion, she accepts offerings of honey in return for sweetening the lives of her beloved devotees through problem-solving and cutting away what is no longer helpful in their lives. This manifestation of Shakti is ruled by Jupiter and is appealed to for marital and progenerative boons amongst others.

Usually riding on a mule comes Kali-like Kalaratri, deity of the seventh day, black as the night and breathing fire, and carrying among her weapons a noose, trident, and sword; she is benign nonetheless. The saturnine Kalaratri protects her supplicants from ghosts and all malign spirits, scaring them away with her own ghoulish righteousness.

In visual contrast to Kalaratri is Durga's form of Mahagauri, resplendent deity who rides a white bull or sometimes elephant, and whose aura flows like gentle, purifying water over all who behold her. She carries a small drum and a trident, again correlating her with the great mystic god Shiva and to the concomitant arts of meditation. As Parvati, the goddess subjected herself to severe penances in order to win the supreme yogi as her husband. Mahagauri spent several years thus employed, losing track of her physical body until she was both skeletal and filthy. Eventually Shiva rewarded her by showering her with sacred water from the Ganga river. It is in this resplendent, wise and reborn aspect that Durga is worshipped as Mahagauri on the eighth day of Navaratri.

The ninth form of Durga is another of her best-known: Siddhidhatri, in which the supernatural powers elicited by her penances and meditation become pronounced. This is Durga in her most spiritual aspect within the world: sitting on a lotus, holding amongst other tools a book and receiving the devotions of all, including the gods themselves. She is the enemy of ignorance and the epitome of perfection. On this day she is often propitiated with a fast.

It is thus evident that Durga personifies of all the power of protective Good in the cosmos. As such she is overwhelming and impossible to define, exacerbating her quality of distance, particularly from the measurements of the world, and from the male or demonic of the species. However, as we can see from her many attributes, she may be approached on a more personal level as Mother of the Universe, Mataji, in her kindly and pleasant aspect, or in one of her warrior manifestations, as an exemplar and champion of inner strength and overriding intelligence.

As mentioned, in some renditions of Durga's scriptures her sole requirement from a suitor is that he must be able to defeat her in battle. Naturally this is impossible and, though entire armies rise to the challenge, she remains unfettered by a husband. Her role as sustainer of cosmic balance ensures that her opponents are primarily demons whose excessive vanity leads them to misjudge Durga's vulnerability to their attack. Although often coupled with Shiva, in her maiden aspect she evinces great latent power and is at prime capacity to aid supplicants.

As wife of Shiva and mother of Skanda, Durga is ally to married women also and is perceived as a wifely role model: her steadfast nature, strength, and wiliness are deemed to honey any household. Conversely, this goddess can be a powerful ally in challenging social stereotypes. She may be broached, for example, for the strength required to remain single or not to have children, which can still, in this theoretically liberated and definitely overpopulated age, be considered unnatural; or in matters challenging traditional ideals of marriage or monogamy, such as the increasingly popular practice of polyamory, or for the fortitude to emerge from the closet and sustain a relationship with a same-sex partner, or to come out as trans, gender-fluid, or nonbinary. Anything that flies in the face of convention, particularly male-imposed convention, may be deemed appropriate to Durga as well as to Kali.

Females are no longer perceived merely in relation to their men—as daughters, wives, and mothers. Durga is a good role model for women, Hindu or otherwise, who wish to burn bright in their own right; particularly those who refuse to compromise the positive points of their femininity to their cause. She symbolizes women who employ every aspect of themselves to get what they want. As such, Durga is a rebel; like Kali, she eats and drinks metaphorical meat and wine (taboo substances to the Hindu), which she is free to do because of her cosmic composition, fashioned from a will to see justice done. Nothing can be impure that touches her divinity: the same applies to the sacred waters of India, some of which are physically toxic and polluted, but which are bathed in and prayed in through good faith despite this. Cosmic purity is ineffable.

Durga provides us with a little indulgence, a little leeway in the cause of a higher good. She refutes parochial ideals and substitutes them with an elegant alternative, always highly original. Durga safeguards the integral individuality of women. For those who wish for a conventional marriage and all that it entails, she is also patroness. She stands indomitable on her fearsome feline steed, and in a cosmic context is said to simultaneously create, maintain, and destroy the world, confirming her to be an amalgam of all deities (Brahma, Vishnu, Shiva). Being in control of reality-levels, she is also the power of sleep, and may be approached for aid in matters pertaining to this, and to astral travel and out of body experiences.

Durga is not, like Kali, implacable once roused; she sympathizes with other standpoints but does her own thing anyway because she knows it to be right. She takes power from the male gods and deceives others with her feminine appearance … and then slays them, but only to preserve dharma, universal balance. She might even be deemed a confrontational version of the Egyptian Ma'at, somewhat comparable to Sekhmet.

Thus, Durga is the ideal goddess to approach when we have a strong sense of overriding justification about something that challenges the less-considered standards of others. Her lightning bolt, thunderbolt, trident, and discus are formidable weapons designed to further the cause of good in the universe; personal rectitude is essential. It is helpful to meditate a while on your cause and fill yourself with indignation before you visualize Durga. Tapping into her character traits will, as with any deity, help you to channel her.

This baffling goddess, with her beauty and her physical power, her modes of action and suspension of activity, her ability to destroy or to heal, may be summarized as an embodiment of fortitude.

It is for this quality that we shall approach her in any of its variants.

Approaching Durga: Preparation

Traditionally, autumn or spring are ideal times to appeal to Durga, the main *Durga Puja* festivals falling in September/October, marking five to ten days of veneration of the goddess. However, we cannot always pick our season, and Durga is omnipresent all through the year, so one might work any time, or with a full moon or just waning, chanting one of her mantras and/or performing some simple bhakti (worship) before an image of the goddess.

Favorite gifts for Durga include blue lotus flowers or replicas thereof, fresh water, incense, pure ghee, flame, sugar, fruits, milk, honey, jaggery, and sesame seeds. Different forms of the goddess traditionally receive particular offerings, but anything given with focus and purity of intent should be suitable. Best of all is the chanting, mentally or aloud, of her mantras and praises.

Visualization for Strength

Once you have created a suitably fiery atmosphere and rightful sense of justice, position yourself comfortably and take a couple of deep golden breaths in, allowing any tension and negativity to exit your body. Continue for as long as needed, until you feel relaxed and receptive.

Begin to visualize this incredibly beautiful, strong, and feminine goddess mounted on her lion, her ten arms fanning around her shoulders with supernatural potential and ability. The tools Durga carries range from a dagger to a discus to a conch shell; in each deceptively slender hand she holds a peace-keeping weapon. Note well, however, her trident and metal discus. See her complete mastery of the beast she rides, symbolizing her absolute transcendence of baser instincts such as greed and lust.

As Durga's image becomes clearer in your mind, feel the quiet respect flowing from you to the goddess. Her discipline and ability are indeed admirable. Mentally bow at her gold-sandaled feet, giving obeisance to the deity whose skills you wish to emulate.

Now, ask Durga for her help. Notice that even the skin of her feet emanates a surreal golden glow; as you look up you see that her robes are as red as blood and richly ornamented with precious glinting gems and burnished metal threads.

Look into her lower eyes. They are dark and bewitching, infinitely beguiling; their softness is counteracted only by the startling emerald green of the third eye above and between them. This eye carries a different message; one of unrelenting determination and sublime detachment. Here, Durga is a beautiful witch, a formidable foe when stirred. Nothing can deter her, for she knows she will always win—something she has proven time and time again. She would not be here still extant and glorious were this not the case.

Sit with the goddess for a while, as long as you wish. Then imagine that you are actually *becoming* her. Smell the slightly ferrous scent of her robes, the sandalwood aroma of her skin. Feel your own increased ability as your arms replicate, each new limb symbolic of a past experience and the knowledge conferred by it. Breathe in more of the golden light that fills the air in the vicinity of the deity; feel it heightening your resolve and strengthening your capability.

Now, concentrate hard on your objective. Consider your achievements in the past—the harder won, the better—and with the help of Durga, determine to add this to the list.

The tingling sensation between your eyebrows is your third eye beginning to glow green.

Continue to inhale the goddess's aura in long, deep breaths, aware of this new psychically active zone on your forehead.

Focus again on your objective: with justified anger you will slay the demons that intend to block your path, transforming them into subservient inoffensives.

With Durga as your guide, tackle your obstacles mentally. Durga is within you; you need make reference to nothing else. You are utterly strong and entirely independent, requiring nobody's aid; you are a goddess in your own right.

Determine, like Durga, to drive the chariot of your own fate—feel your own aura begin to glow yellow and then red with determination, strength, and hope. Keep breathing in and assimilating these emotions and colors; pack them into your psychic battery for future use.

When you exhale, you emit in smoky whorls any weaknesses or cowardice from your soul.

Durga

Charge yourself with surprise reserves of strength. Now, when your tirelessly sanguine persona is fully established and your will is as hard as iron, make moves to confront your obstacles. Do not forget to employ your considerable charms in your cause. The sooner you can approach the situation of enmity, the better.

Make sure you look and feel good, and hold the image of yourself as fearless warrior Durga in your mind. Use to optimum capacity the beauty you know you possess, inner and outer. Keep your aura golden; if any situation turns nasty, you can always switch it to red, but maintain your composure.

Mentally project the image of yourself as Durga at the negative situation. If your problem or obstacle is epitomized by a specific person, do so at their third eye area. Do not allow their words or actions, however harsh, to ruffle your image of your strong, independent Durga-self.

State your case or do your thing, as appropriate. Chances are they will not be able to resist. But even if they do, you know you'll win—because Durga always does.

CHAPTER 3

KALI

In a temple in Dakshineswar, a young yogi is praying devoutly before a stone image of Kali. For many hours on the scorching floor he has meditated, yearning and calling again and again to the divine mother, awaiting her animation in his inner vision, a sure sign of her audience.

Eventually, she rewards his faith. Her third eye clicks open, glaring down on him, veined by blood. She smiles, her lips a noose about his astral body; her fangs yawning, yellow, putrid.

One by one her limbs begin to move; a dark and potent light flows from her head, her four arms, her fulsome body. Stepping down from her lofty altar she slinks toward the prostrate devotee, her necklace of heads human and demonic swinging to and fro, her skirt of severed arms arresting all possibility of kinetic action.

Kali's hand hovers about the yogi's smiling head and touches it on the crown. A lightning bolt of spiritual enlightenment shatters his former illusions: his ego is dissolved. The yogi's boon is granted.

Aum Kring Kring Kring Mahakalikye Namaha

KALI IS THE APOTHEOSIS of nature. She is therefore the embodiment of duality: with two hands she gives; with two she destroys. She is as frightening as she is inevitable; like death, disease, demise, none can escape her. She gives finite form to the eternal soul and must necessarily break the vessel too. Often depicted dancing wildly, her skin might be deep celestial blue or black as the night sky, both demonstrating her infinite nature, her transcendence of the material universe.

Kali guards against complacency; who would fail to take precautions with such a fierce, demanding goddess breathing down one's neck? Pride and materialism become impossible when Kali is present. She destroys injustice and wreaks revenge on the enemies of cosmic law, on the cruel, the materialistic, the megalomaniacal. Along with Durga, she is frequently turned to for protection from one's enemies … and even for their destruction.

As *Mahakali*, the great goddess manifests with ten arms carrying an array of weapons and a severed human head representing her as enemy of the human ego, that which prevents us from attaining *moksha*, or spiritual bliss. Her tongue lolls or flicks and her eyes are red with craving for the blood of demons that might do mischief to humanity, her children.

In the *Devi Mahatmya* texts, Kali fights with Durga and the Matrikas, the "divine mothers" or embodied shakti powers, against the great demon Mahishasura and *phat!*—they slay him. This episode is auspiciously chanted during Durga's festival, Navaratri: Kali is sometimes said to spring from Durga's forehead, the goddess epitomizing benevolence at its most bellicose.

As an embodiment of the wrath of more benign goddesses, Parvati for example, Kali represents justified anger. She is brought into being to destroy demons, usually beings who have performed formidable penances, gained boons of the gods, and then abused their power. The laws of spiritual physics can work counter-intuitively in Hindu scriptures, with motive being discounted and actions themselves registered, perhaps in order to reflect the physical world of *maya* and *samsara* in which corruption is all too often rewarded—at least temporarily.

Together Kali and Durga also face Raktabja, who is able to replicate himself when wounded; his name means "blood seed." In a similar manner to the Egyptian Sekhmet, Kali becomes intoxicated by justified bloodlust. Prior to her arrival at the battle against Raktabja, the demon had been able to produce a thousand warriors from his own essence. With such an army springing from his every injury he was of course insurmountable, a threat to divine order and certainly to mankind. Incensed by his arrogance, mild Parvati—Durga—manifests from her forehead the all-consuming Kali, who drinks every drop of Raktabja's blood before it has the power to reproduce, leaving him a drained husk. So great is her pleasure in this that her death-dance threatens the stability of the universe itself.

In desperation the gods call upon her consort Shiva to help. He tries, but his pleas do not reach Kali: it is not until he prostrates himself on the battlefield and she realizes she is trampling on the chest of her own beloved husband that Kali stops, hence the famous image. In some versions she is depicted with right foot forward: this is *Bhadra Kali*, a more civilized version of the goddess. Those who adhere to the "left hand" Tantric path worship her as *Smashan-Kali*; with her left foot forward, she of chaos, wild nature and cremation ground. This striking iconography is symbolic of Shiva as primeval cosmic consciousness and Kali as time, dancing upon this foundation and causing civilizations to rise and fall. Her wrath is entirely immune to the specifics of personality or personal desire, for she destroys the body and all that goes with it, eventually bringing total liberation from desire. This is rather ironic as many of her worshippers, being often of the poorer classes, are desirous of money, power, and land. It is widely understood that appealing to Kali for such boons is a risky business and may backfire for one's own greater good. It is much safer to approach Lakshmi for the luxuries of life.

In one version in the Puranas, the sweet-natured maternal aspect of the goddess, manifest as Uma, drinks the poison stored in Shiva's throat in order to become Kali and thus fight the rampant demon Daruka, who again can only be killed by a woman. Naturally Kali becomes intoxicated by her bloody victory, and this time can only be halted when Shiva manifests as a small boy crying in a nearby cemetery. Reverting to her role as loving mother, Kali halts and brings him her breast to suckle. Shiva thus draws out the poison, and her peaceful nature is restored.

Kali is also depicted with four arms, and sometimes with ten heads, able to look in all directions at once: and into many different dimensions, as does Mahashiva in his multiheaded form. In Hinduism we are always reminded that our material reality is just one of many extant reality-truths. Life exists outside and well beyond human conception and sense-perception, on different levels, planets, and in realms invisible to the naked eye. The gods, of course, are fluent in these multifarious wavelengths.

Although she is most popularly deemed a goddess of destruction, the principles of creation and preservation also lie in Kali's domain, for she is the great mother. She sometimes rides a lion, and her tools include the tripscula or trident, a super-sharp sword of divine knowledge, a bowl of fire for purification, and another to catch the blood from the severed head that swings from one of her clenched fists. Often she wears a skirt or girdle of severed arms of her enemies, which dangle uselessly and fill one with revulsion for the human mindset and its temporary pleasures.

To the yogi, Kali is God made manifest in Mother Nature: her hair unbound and her gestures wild and free, the mystic knows God to be eternally graceful and creative. Sometimes she wears a tiger skin, showing her connection with the wilds; other times she is naked, divinely unencumbered by worldly pride or concerns. She is *Kali Ma*, the fearsome mother. To a being already attuned to immortality, Kali in all her gore and terror represents the fleeting and liberating experience of being reborn into spirit, and consequently, is not to be feared, but welcomed. This subjective reality of Kali as beneficent is made manifest in her enlightening aspect. She may look terrifying, but her devotee/child understands this to be a blessing. Consequently, the great goddess blesses her creations.

The message underlying Kali's iconography is that we are not merely flesh and that creation is not merely material. It is for this reason that those following her spiritual path in India are encouraged to meditate at night, in a graveyard or cremation ground, naked, with disheveled hair, refuting cleanliness, chanting Kali's mantra. Extreme *aghoris*, dedicants of Kali and Shiva, eat only what can be scavenged from refuse or from the funeral pyre itself: the consumption of abandoned human flesh and animal feces representing, as well as self-mortification, the sacredness of all, pointedly including that which is taboo, diseased, pestilential, and anathema to ordinary sensibilities. Such terrifyingly extreme disciplines are not for the lay person, yet there is something of the principle of familiarity breeds contempt in the ordinary worshipper spending a night amidst corpses, scavenging creatures, mourners, and ghosts; the scariest dark night is lived through—demons may well run riot in the mind and specters terrorize the soul—but one is still extant in the morning to tell the tale: hopefully having gleaned a vision of this darkest of goddesses and enlightenment about the transitory nature of our lives in the illusion of maya.

The cremation ground and battlefields are thus Kali's main domain; she is normally depicted surrounded by dead and dying bodies, dancing on these if not upon Shiva's prostrate form. The severed head and bloodied sword she holds exhibit her role as supreme energy responsible for the dissolution of ego.

Kali, like Shiva, goes sky-clad, or naked; she is quite literally divinity unveiled, beyond the bounds of maya, or delusion. Her wild hair and death-dance, her embracing of all that is feared by humanity, represents her limitless freedom. In Hinduism, creative sound is the source of all manifestations (hence partly the great significance of mantras); by wearing a necklace of sometimes human heads, representative of the fifty-two letters of the Sanskrit alphabet and the loss of the physical on death, Kali symbolically suspends the creative and intellectual capacity; at other times her gory *mala*, or garland, features 108 severed craniums, a most propitious number with which to chant an ego-decimating mantra.

Correlating to Kali as *shakti* is the form of Shiva known as *Kala/Kalab-hairava*, another terrifying-looking fanged incarnation meaning both "black" and "time." The horrors of the Tantric blood pit sacred to them are those of the void in which worldly knowledge and power cease to have any meaning: ego is successfully destroyed. Likewise, Kali's skirt of arms indicates the cessation of physical activity, that which makes us seem alive and part of society. In Kali, our lives are suspended between worlds. She represents both death and the period between incarnations when the shock of death still lingers. She is the reigning goddess of traumatic transitions.

As well as epitomizing the numinous qualities of blackness, the name Kali denotes the origin of limited power. Through the volition of time, every life—no matter how wealthy or powerful a person may be—is cauterized, made finite. Time is the great equalizer. On one hand, Shiva's prostration under Kali's feet indicates the power of higher emotions within the psyche of the goddess, even at its most negative; on the other it shows her as the dynamic shakti-energy of Shiva or Brahman, without which they would be beyond thought and action, and too lofty for the world of mortals. Kali's root is in eternity, but she defines our material reality. What Shiva dreams, Kali realizes and sets into motion. Thus we see that all energies, all lifeforms and godforms act in reference to other energies and beings. Nothing is separate, all is one, *aum*.

Sadly, human so-called civilization and patriarchal values do little to reflect this balance. In India, where female infanticide, high maternal mortality, domestic violence, rape, and the neglect of women's health means that more than sixty million women are statistically missing from society—sociologically void, voiceless, and abused—justified anger as expressed by a female deity is more than a little appropriate. Indeed, it is surprising that so few cultures can boast a fearsome, protective female deity, considering the sorry state of women's rights globally. It is apt that Kali is a popular symbol for the worldwide women's movement. As divine nature, she refutes all that is unnatural to the soul. She is an ideal goddess to whom to appeal to help terminate cycles of abuse.

Kali herself reveals the presence of chaos and rebellion; she may choose to elevate or to destroy—her decision must be trusted implicitly. As all-powerful nature and the justice of cosmic balance, there is no going against her. The best we can do is relax and appreciate the ride. The benighted devotee sitting in the ashes of the dead undergoes trepidation, fights the fear, dissolves into it with what might be termed a sort of blissful stoicism, and eventually transcends it. They emerge in the morning (hopefully) devoid of fear of death. They realize that they are already dead, and that the so-called dead are already living. Kali-Kala-Time is an illusion. All is Now.

With the sum of the present as the sole relevant factor, we must either trust, or die of fear. Like many areas of Hinduism, the Kali philosophy encourages a certain liberating fatalism. Kali says, "face the terror and do it anyway." She encourages her devotees to combat their ghouls by bringing them into the light of conscious recognition. In giving reference to the fear, she challenges complacency; by exhibiting destruction as a part of cosmic order, she helps us overcome it. There is much of benefit to be gained from this apparently monstrous divinity.

Still, by most modern standards, the animal and child sacrifice usually erroneously associated with Kali worship take this principle a little too far. Kali is indeed a goddess to whom animals may be ritually slaughtered if one wishes to eat meat—a practice widely condemned in the Vedas—but the accompanying mantra that must be chanted whilst slitting the animal's throat translates as: "In the next life, I will be you, and you will be me!" Thus, clearly the abuse of animals and eating of meat is heavily discouraged, and one's gluttony or pride in a special occasion would have to be vast to overcome this proviso. In addition, it is said to be Kali's ghostly consort animals and spirits that consume such offerings: her jackals, ghouls and goblins, not the goddess herself.

The spilling of blood in puja is anathema to Vedic lore, and besides is arguably spiritually symbolic in import, just as Abraham's near-sacrifice of his son Isaac in the Bible demonstrates total obedience to God and the willingness to relinquish that which is dearest to him. Happily, in Hinduism, a coconut is split open to represent the blood/milk of life.

When Kali drinks blood or eats flesh, it is for a higher cosmic purpose, never for personal pleasure. The sanitized version of Kali popular in the West, however, is inaccurate. Kali is a bloody goddess whose tongue does not loll for nothing; her major function is to scare us into remembrance of our divine nature. She is anti-ego; that is, against the preciousness of ego. Approaching her is always a risk, and she will respond with a challenge.

While contemplating Kali, you will most likely find that issues pertaining to any abuse you have suffered, particularly sexual abuse, will come to the fore. Fears and phobias are other probable themes. Other goddesses are plain sailing compared to the profound upheavals Kali can bring.

Kali causes one to fight; having experienced her, one's personal strength is indubitable because the challenge has been faced and victory, psychological and/or physical, has been won. She can aid the termination of cycles of abuse by substituting a victim mentality with that of wisdom and self-preservation. Through knowledge of one's own value and paradoxically of the irrelevance of our tiny slice of perception, Kali transforms what seems to be negative into radiant strength. With Kali, to have visited the battlefields of the cosmic forces and to have paid personal witness to the struggle between light and darkness is a positive virtue. One cannot fight the dark side until one really knows its essence; the experience, though terrorizing at the time, is ultimately an act of empowerment.

Overcoming Cycles of Abuse

The way we react to abusive situations can define our lives. Some employ past abuse, emotional, physical, or circumstantial, as a (possibly unconscious) excuse for all personal failings; modern psychology even encourages a victim syndrome by turning it into a sustainable industry requiring endless rehashes of the past in its misguided concept of therapy, and/or chemical intervention. Others gain incredible strength and self-respect when they emerge from adversity sane and spiritually whole, able to move on without feeling the need to continually reinvoke the negative past—something that takes time and effort. There is a balance between being too precious about oneself—"I'd rather *die* or kill than have someone so much as lay a finger on me without my consent"—and the sort of low self-esteem one encounters in sufferers of habitual domestic violence—"I deserve it; I was asking for it really." There is also the issue of admitting, either consciously or out loud, that one is being abused.

The three initial steps one must take to end abuse are: conscious recognition, acquisition of self-esteem, and determination to fight the maltreatment.

Unfortunately, all are easier said than done. Enlightenment cannot be forced. In some cases, people choose to be prisoners in order to find out the hard way the purpose of their time on this planet, convoluted as this may seem. That suffering is not a necessity, is a concept still to be learned by many on this plane. We hopefully learn from suffering, but we do not have to suffer to learn.

Of course, most of us in the current era are aware and willing to admit when we have been abused, particularly if this was physical as well as emotional. It may have taken place in the distant past, such as childhood, or even, as some believe, in another life, but perhaps its memory surfaces at inopportune times; for example, if the abuse was sexual and it infringes on current physical relations. Maybe recurrent dreams, nightmares, or feeling a general malaise are underlining latter-day feelings of helplessness, of being trapped by the past. Often post-traumatic stress disorder springs from these events, as can agoraphobia, eating disorders, social anxiety disorder, and many other blights. The manifestations are countless will likely affect the physical body as well as the mind, but in undergoing a purgative exercise such as the following with Kali, at least some of the karmic miasma should be lifted.

In the case of physical abuse, those who claim they would never allow it to happen to them and would positively murder any potential encroacher are being insensitive to the millions of victims who never stood a chance. It is easy to stand back and fantasize perpetual integrity or feats of bravery in a crisis; it is quite another to manage them against all physical odds.

Although caution over one's safety is essential, we must not allow fear, gratuitous or otherwise, to dominate our lives. Indeed, what greater infringement could there possibly be on our liberty? Personal responsibility—not self-blame—is the key. We are all fundamentally alone on this plane and it is unwise to rely on other people, as some women do on their men, for protection. Circumstances dictate that there are things we can do and things we cannot. As Kali likes to remind us, we are each mortal, including those who abuse and attack; and although we may feel big in our little worlds, in many ways we are all fragile. As Mahakali also indicates along with Durga, there are surprising reserves of strength behind the delusion of frailty. This may sound like a mixed message, but it is easily translated. Take optimum care of yourself; be brave; be true unto yourself and to the powers of justice, and in return the goddess will take optimum care of you.

When we enter Kali's cosmic spiral, we say goodbye to our precious sense of ego and are utterly humbled, like so many of those born into her service. Most of Kali's native worshippers belong to low-caste communities in which pride is as unlikely a character trait as humility is to a Bollywood superstar in Mumbai. Kali is ego-death—the force that equalizes irrespective of social status or personal or borrowed power—hence her decapitated victims with their faculties and tools no longer to hand, each equal to the other. Many folk who have "died" or who have had a near-death experience entirely lose their fear of the process; indeed, some look forward to reexperiencing the uplifting spiritual calm they feel on passing through the dimensions. Likewise, we can lose our fear of everything Kali represents once we have experienced and passed through it. Dissolution is not such a terrible thing; there are many more wonders on the other side of the veil.

When working with any Hindu god, it is always a good idea to begin by meditating one of their mantras. The Sanskrit language is deeply magickal and serves to get your brain on the right wavelength, as well as being pleasing to the deity concerned. Mantras range from the extremely complex (at least to Western sensibilities) to the simple. One such for Kali is *Aum Kring Mahakali Kaliye Namaha*; it is usual practice to repeat this 108 times.

Please note again that all of these visualizations are intended to give the reader ideas for themselves and can be extrapolated upon and personalized. Do what feels right and brings effects for you as an individual.

Visualization for Ending Cycles of Abuse: Part One

Light one black, one red, and one white candle, in that order. If music helps you visualize, play something that reminds you of the situation you are intending to recover from or terminate; if you prefer something less personal, anything fierce and melodramatic is ideal.

Contemplate the abuse you have undergone; the cycle you wish to break. Allow yourself to become angry and upset. The more intense your feelings, the more powerful the visualization will be. Resolve to terminate that which is causing your grief, to pull out the pins even if you feel they are part of the structure of your psyche. This means changing the way you think, removing reoccurring thought-patterns and memories and avoiding the people and places that provoke them. Steel yourself in readiness to extricate yourself from the situation, both literally and mentally.

Now, breathe in and out three times. As you do so, imagine red light filling your lungs and permeating your body. Continue to think of the scenarios that have caused you so much pain. As you do this, the brightness of the red encasing you increases.

Gradually, you feel your blood being fortified by superhuman strength.

It is the strength of justice, and it seems to be swelling in your body and mind, permeating every aspect of your being. You begin to feel indomitable, and as the blood pumps quickly through your veins you notice that your aura has grown spiky and is extending in ferocious points from your body.

Now, focus on the flame of the black candle and imagine it receding beneath you, so you are viewing it from an ever-increasing altitude. As you look down at it, you notice a necklace of fleshy, bleeding skulls hanging down to your waist, and a skirt of severed arms about your hips.

Imagine, dancing around the black candle far below you, tiny caricatures of the people who have abused you emotionally, mentally, or physically. Concentrate on their diminutive forms until they are well established in your mind and allow your thoughts to turn to bloodlust. This is your chance to get even.

Make your presence known to the soon-to-be victims of your retribution. As you tower above their cowering forms, swiping at them and decapitating them as a cat might batter a bluebottle, be aware of yourself as literally above the situation. Whatever they have done to you in the past has not cast you low, but rather, raised you high above them all. You are a proud survivor!

Return mentally to the scene of the abuse, and *be* your new, empowered persona. Recall the moment of crisis, then turn on them as you are now. Shock them. Frighten them as they did you.

Really let yourself go with this childlike catharsis. If you can, use physical actions to accompany your visualizations.

As you launch your attack, punch the air or a pillow, or tear a pad of paper as if it were their flesh—indulge your imagination. Your power is limitless; do unto others as they did unto you. This is your safe space, your own

Kali

sacred sphere of protection. Effect your own judgment, your long-awaited retribution. Know that the gods are watching and that your actions are influencing your abusers-turned-victims astrally; there can be no doubt that with every lashing you give them their power is diminished. Blow out the black candle, the center of their power.

In comes Kali. You look a lot like her so her grisly appearance does not frighten you; she is your sister in battle. As a matter of fact, you seem to be merging with her—you now have four arms with which to effect your revenge and a tongue positively made to lick up blood!

Tear your demons to pieces. They are attached to you and easily accessed through your aura. Follow the bloody cords and rip them as if murdering some unwanted offspring. You may have bred this pestilence, it may have become embroiled with you, but you no longer want to be affiliated with it. Kill it!

Continue in your death-dance for as long as you feel inspired. When you are quite satisfied that the negative entities have been sundered from your person, and you are happy with your retributive carnage, incinerate the "bodies" in the purifying fire of the white candle flame. Imagine yourself committing the mangled remains of your abusers to the fire of peace. When you are ready, mentally cauterize your own wounds with the white candle's light. Imagine it sealing your body and spirit to exclude further infringements on your person.

Come out of this emotional ordeal whenever you feel ready and blow out the red candle. Return to the process whenever the mettle in your soul is rusting. Remember that justified anger is not karmically debilitating but entirely necessary. Do not feel bad about feeling bad. Kill the cycle of abuse before it kills you.

If you have been listening to music as you purge, either switch it off now or change to a soothing soundtrack, something light and fresh. Blow out the black candle. Wrap the two used candles in a piece of black cloth and take the white one, still lit, into the bathroom with you for part 2 of the process.

Ending Cycles of Abuse: Part 2

By the light of your remaining white candle, fill the bath with warm water. You may like to light some more white candles to brighten the bathroom as you bathe. Light a stick of sandalwood incense and waft it around the room and over your naked body.

Now, hold a fistful of preferably Himalayan or sea salt skyward and visualize it glowing a brilliant cleansing blue-white. Scatter this into the stream of tap water and watch the luminescence spread to every atom of bathwater.

When the water looks a glowing white to your inner vision, step in. Immerse yourself fully in the cleansing waters, conscious of letting the unclean matter of your past dissolve and flake away as you do so. Allow the negativity you previously felt to seep out of your body and into the water, leaving you calm and relaxed. The memories of the experiences you underwent are transforming themselves into positive strengths; your body is glowing with the white fire of initiation.

Having fought in battle and emerged victorious, you may now consider yourself a warrior to be reckoned with. As you float your body in the purification bath, allow your mind to roam and survey the expanse of your experience. Feel proud of yourself for having survived when many would have fallen by the wayside.

Splash your bodies—physical, astral, and emotional—with the purifying waters until no residue of your bloody confrontation remains. Take several deep, slow breaths, in and out, knowing that you have finally released yourself from the cycle of abuse. You have fought your bullies and won. In all future battles, you will have Kali on your side. Having been there and done that, and with the goddess's assistance, you have nothing further to fear. You have crossed the abyss, confronted the worst that is possible to face—you can never be vulnerable again, with this wealth of experience behind you.

Award yourself a gift of courage, and determine never to let such a situation arise again. However, if it should, you know you could cope. Above all else, you have a sanctum of inner purity that nothing and nobody can defile.

Arise radiant from your bath when you feel ready.

As the last of the water spirals down the drain carrying with it the last of your grief and fear, know yourself to be thoroughly cleansed of the past. The future is all yours now. You have passed the tests and graduated into a higher awareness. The ghouls have been conquered and your life is your playground.

Kali

It is very important to keep your own mind-forged bullies at bay from now on: that is, the habits of thought that have become regular loops in your brain. Every time you find yourself dwelling on the same now-obsolete memories and thought-patterns, dismiss them. Do not allow others to draw you back onto the topic, and, as much as you can, avoid people, locations, music, images, clothes, even scents that carry you down that old labyrinth. Your life has changed—you have moved on. Resolve to relish this new chapter.

After extinguishing the white candle, put anything of it that remains with the red and black candles. Snap the black candle in half and declare: "Enemy mine, your curse has failed to taint me!"

Tie all the pieces together in the black cloth and bury them somewhere far away from your home.

Repeat whole or in part as much as is needed.

Overcoming Phobias

Phobias are as fascinating as they are inconvenient. The illogical impulse of terror when confronted by a spider, a feather, or a body of water, for example, tells us a great deal about our present psychology and often our past lives. Phobias may be analyzed symbolically to interesting effect: hydrophobes, for example, are often overly self-controlled, refusing to experiment or let themselves go; they likewise refuse to float on the waters of life, to go with the flow. Water being a symbol of emotion, they are essentially afraid of the strength of their own feelings, frightened they will be overwhelmed if they stop standing guard at the floodgates. On one level, the hydrophobe may have simply drowned in a previous incarnation (most of us have, at some point; it is when the death is particularly emotionally painful or untimely that we tend to recall it); most likely, the victim is subconsciously relating this experience to the concerns already mentioned. A repressive upbringing with a domineering mother figure and possible physical violence are usually the psychological backdrops to this particular phobia.

Analysis, however, is not always the answer. Accepting that there is a reason for the fear does not necessarily dispel it; deep-rooted neuroses take time and reprogramming before they cease to be unruly. Sometimes knowing the phobia is illogical (such as fear of something that cannot harm you) can actually make it worse, so trying to reason it away can be detrimental. Repeating a visualization once with huge impact or multiple times can, however, do much to soothe the subconscious and stem illogical fear at the source. Familiarity breeds contempt if one wills it so. It is worth interpreting phobias for their spiritual symbolism and the startling insights one may glean from these bizarre aversions, but it feels good to shed them. Nobody likes to be shackled by uncontrollable impulses; unless, of course, they are seeking attention by being hysterical. In most cases, however, the phobia is entirely genuine and, if you are contemplating this exercise, you clearly wish to be released from it.

A goddess is not specifically mentioned in this visualization in order to keep the process relatively simple. Instead, I use a scenario that actually happened to me while I was in Thailand contemplating Kali. Even though she is not mentioned specifically, the principles and events derive directly from her, and the experience befits the goddess's role of strength-bearer in adversity, as well as challenger of fearfulness. It is on these grounds that the following exercise has been formulated.

Visualization for Overcoming Phobias

There is no need to employ yogic breathing prior to this exercise. If you encounter your phobia in the street, you will not have time for such self-calming tactics; best to approach it *au naturel* as you would in the wild, so to speak.

Decide on whom you wish to take with you on this inner journey. You can choose a friend, a partner, or an expression of your future self—the part of you not shackled by such considerations as phobias or other ailments. If you feel attuned to this Higher Self, a visualization concerning that person will be extremely positive. Whomever you choose, they will be referred to in the exercise as "X."

Also, if you have more than one phobia, decide which one you wish to deal with first. It is best to handle your fears one at a time. You can repeat this exercise another time using another phobia if you so desire.

Imagine yourself in a jungle. You have been walking for some time, following an old mud track you hope will lead to civilization, or at least to something interesting. It is extremely hot. You are in a holiday mood, enjoying the opportunity to explore the tropical island you're visiting; you are aware of being quite a long way from your shack.

So far, you have crossed several plantations, and in one of these you passed the most enormous bull you've ever seen. Its scythe-like horns were lowered, but luckily, not in aggression. The formidable bovine was busy at its meal of luscious grass.

You are enjoying the scenery, especially in the company of X. You are chatting about the flora and fauna and wondering how likely it is to be knocked unconscious by a falling coconut.

You come to a narrow part of the track. X takes the lead; you lag a little, admiring the tropical scenery. Sweat drips down your face, back, and legs. The humidity is stifling.

There is a significant gap between the two of you now.

Looking ahead, assessing your route, you are startled to notice a body-sized pit in your immediate path. Gazing in, you are horrified to behold a profusion of your phobia lying in the gap, directly between you and X.

Allow yourself to be saturated by your emotional response, yet be aware of the overview—this is all imaginary, an illusion.

Adhering to that objectivity as best you can, you gaze into the abyss, your instinct to run almost curtailed by the petrification you feel.

A noise behind you makes you turn.

The bull you passed earlier is heading your way, and at speed. You either brave the phobia-filled abyss, or end your days as a human kebab.

X, on the other side, is bidding you act with speed. They suggest you stare into their eyes as you take the leap over the living symbols of your phobia. With the heavy thud of hooves thundering at your tail, you have very little time to make the choice.

Adrenaline coursing through your veins, you jump. It is not easy, but you force yourself to do it. Behind you, the bull halts at the pit. X embraces you in relief.

Repeat this visualization until you are thoroughly acquainted with the idea and image of the thing that scares you, and you do not hesitate to make the leap of faith. Repeat it until you know that, in real life, you would do the same thing fearlessly, metaphorical bull or no bull.

❦

Chapter 3

CHAPTER 4

LAKSHMI

Lakshmi spreads her sails across the Hindu pantheon, stately as a ship coming into dock laden with gold, spices, and finely crafted jewels. Her cargo is burnished with a holy luster: her gifts are for the royal and priestly, the noble and devout; her stories are of enterprise and virtuous behavior. This Empress's sons are rulers whose authority springs from diplomacy rather than force, for mounted on their gem-bedecked elephants and pungent with foreign spice-oils, they quell the peasants by presence alone, and all who see them call them demigods.

Lakshmi, mild and rich as butter, sits and smiles. Blesser of brides and consecrator of marriages, she guards the cream of life, pouring it into the upheld jugs of those who please her, curdling that of those who do not. Ghee lamps shine in her honor, attracting Lakshmi's luck into the house. If her devotees are truly blessed, she will inhabit their very bodies; their faces will glow with beauty, their deepest wishes will come true.

It is Lakshmi's sweet blessing that makes of an incarnation a delicious morsel of consciousness.

Aum Shreem Maha Lakshmiyei Namaha
Aum Shreem Shree-aee Namaha

LAKSHMI IS DEPICTED IN the Hindu scriptures as the Goddess of Status, Wealth, and Sovereignty, all of which makes her an extremely popular deity, needless to say. She is a household goddess worshipped all over India, usually alongside her consort Vishnu, or Narayan (Krishna); she is pleased by their worship in addition to her own. Her name means "sign," "to perceive and observe," suggesting flowing with the cosmic tides and judging what is auspicious at which point; she is also known by the title of *Sri,* meaning "prosperity." Her unchallenging nature (as opposed to that of, say, Kali or Durga), her calm, loving manner, and the ease with which her blessing is attained mean she is pleasant and effective to supplicate.

Lakshmi is appealed to by modern Hindus for *artha* (wealth, fortune), as well as for fifteen other forms of prosperity including fame, courage, and intelligence; as well as victory, good health, morality, good offspring, gems, and gold—essentially everything deemed necessary for an affluent, successful incarnation. She is frequently depicted framed by golden coins and with money flowing from her palms, which are always open, always giving. The recipients of her boons are likewise encouraged to be openhanded with their wealth.

Lakshmi has regal elephants as her consorts, symbols of strength and majesty. Often the noble beasts are showering her with water from their trunks, representing health, refreshment, and the creative powers conferred by water.

Chapter 4

She is associated with light and its qualities, and candles are often lit to engender her favor. In this aspect, Lakshmi exhibits a yellowy, ghee-colored complexion and aura, denoting well-being and nourishment.

Her other gifts include a form of *moksha*, or beauty; *kama*, which is supreme love and carnal pleasure; and *dharma*, or righteousness. In the case of the first two, the goddess develops a pink hue denoting compassion and femininity; when appealed to for loftier purposes such as dharmic balance, she becomes the radiant white of the cosmic intelligence itself. It is in this aspect that we recognize her connection with the other goddesses—particularly Saraswati (there is much sisterly rivalry between these two, however) and Radha, who is purported to be an avatar of Lakshmi when Vishnu is incarnate as Krishna—and perceive on less specific terms the all-pervasive, motivating force behind them.

Often Lakshmi sits on a lotus in a pose indicative of transcendence of earthly ties. She is surrounded by buds and blooms in various stages of development, representing the various stages of the creation of the universe. Here we witness her in the ubiquitous role of cosmic creator; all goddesses have a hand in the origins of life, and Lakshmi the fertility-bearer is key to this. She is capable of manifesting in numerous forms; in the *Bhagavata Purana*, for example, Krishna marries sixteen thousand wives, all of them manifestations of Lakshmi. When she first emerges in Hindu myth, she is compellingly beautiful and desired, and she and Vishnu spend a great deal of time making love, underlining her progenitive properties.

She carries with her a pot of *amrita*, the bliss-juice of immortality churned from the seas of Indian mythology, with which she can grant karma and bestow ecstatic states. In another hand she bears a bilva or bael fruit, rather sensually unappealing, but an elixir of health used in ayurveda and sacred in Hinduism. The bilva symbolizes spiritual strife—moksha in its highest form. Although popularly portrayed in Indian painting as the personification of beauty, the beatitude Lakshmi can grant is not merely physical.

Her other properties, such as wealth and royal power, symbolized by other hands bearing such paraphernalia as a conch shell, an arrow, or golden coins, are each sublimated through the influence of divine will and spiritual awareness, manifesting as a lotus blossom. Bearing this in mind, Lakshmi is the matron goddess of *meaningful* wealth; that is, what we need in order to achieve our life's ambitions, plus a little to play with. As has been numerously pointed out over the past decades, ours is an era in which following one's heart can manifest rewards of all natures, including of course the material. The time to be coy about comfort—or feel guilty for it—is passed, compassion and generosity withstanding.

Traditionally, Lakshmi's boons are sought through *vratas*, tasks of devotion usually enacted during festivals, for which the goddess will, if pleased, grant rewards. In Hindu mythology, even demons can, and frequently do, gain incredible powers by performing grueling feats of self-sacrifice and endurance; inevitably, they show their true colors once their boon has been granted, and Durga or Kali or some other righteous slayer has to be brought in to sort them out. This principle indicates, however, that no matter how bad one's past, one can still curry the favor of the great ones and attempt a virtuous life. In Hinduism it is never too late to change. Because of the appealing nature of her gifts, comprising everything from large incomes to marital fidelity and fertility, Lakshmi receives a great deal of devotional penance and abnegation. However, like all worldly fortune itself, Lakshmi is fickle, flickering, unsteady—*chanchala,* one of her Sanskrit epithets. She must be worshipped alongside the preserver of creation, Vishnu; selfish motives alone will fail.

Puja to Lakshmi is a fundamental element of most Hindu lives. Typically the supplicant is seated on a prayer-cloth in an area cleansed by sprinkling holy water, facing north/northeast/east, the most auspicious directions. The twenty-seven steps of Lakshmi puja include the application of sacred powders such as kumkum to one's third eye and to statues of the gods, meditation on the divine, the offering of a seat (this can be done with flowers or in even more diminutive form), ritual libations; a bath, water to drink, sacred thread, and many different foodstuffs. Coconuts are used in Hindu ritual in lieu of live sacrifice: the milk of the coconut comes from a nonviolent source and is thus much better than blood. Sandalwood and sweet perfumes are offered, and light in the form of flame, and the names of the deity, her scriptural stories and her mantras are chanted in devotions usually numbering 108.

As with all actions, the goddess Lakshmi has an equal and opposite reaction, embodied by her sister Alakshmi. Alakshmi represents misfortune and regret, hexes, poor health, and ugliness, and can be found in icon form in some temples, a crooked hag riding an ass. It is an interesting angle of Hinduism that no aspect of human misery is ever ignored; rather, its divine representatives are to be appeased with worship and prayer with the intention to keep them away. During the Diwali festival, when demons run amok and pecuniary abandon is encouraged, images of Alakshmi may be found in some temples in place of those of her sister. At the end of the festival the unlucky crone is evicted by use of fire-torches and a cacophony of pots and pans, or she has her nose and ears broken, symbolizing the breaking of her malignant spell. Beautiful Lakshmi is reinstated and a new cycle begins. Accordingly, she also represents new beginnings, recuperative properties, and protection from evil.

Visualization for Spiritual and Material Well-Being

For this meditation we approach Lakshmi in her golden, wholesome aspect. She brings the ultimate wealth—happiness—and from this flows the props of life: food, shelter, health. She encourages us to look behind the veil and recognize that all earthly manifestations have their origins in the spiritual realms. The fruits of the earth plane come directly from the astral and spiritual spheres—and we influence these by our own thought-vibrations. By channeling our desires through Lakshmi we can clarify and define them, and make it easier for our positive thoughts to return to us in specific, solid form.

The following mediation involves visualizing a garden, park or natural beauty spot, and it will help if you decide prior to the exercise what your surroundings will look like. The scenery should reflect your state of mind. If life seems difficult to you at the moment, let it be winter, with sparse greenery and stark, leafless trees. If things are looking up, choose spring with small flowers emerging and trees in bud. If you are already feeling pretty good, you should visualize the verdure and color of early summer. Dress the scene up or down accordingly but be sure to leave plenty of room for future embellishment.

Sit cross-legged on the floor or bed, or however you are most comfortable, take several long, deep breaths, and imagine yourself sitting in the same position outside. You are possibly sitting beneath a peepul or banyan tree, or it may be a cool pine or a spreading oak—choose one that best fits your mood.

Before you is a lake, its surface ruffling reflections of the sky; a few lotus petals are floating on it. Looking around, you notice the season. Admire your scenery and imagine how lovely it will look at the height of its flourishing in summer, and how you too will be full of health and happiness by that time with no material concerns to drain you.

Now the vision becomes flat. The three-dimensionality has gone, and you realize you can peel the entire scene away like a freshly glued poster. Catch a corner and pull it upward to reveal the brilliant yellow light behind. This light seems thick and nourishing; you can touch as well as see and smell it. Each particle glows with inner radiance, and the overall effect entrances you. You realize that there is light behind everything: an all-pervasive essence of expansive, conscious compassion.

As you think this, your original image of the park becomes superimposed on the yellowy radiance; you witness both scenes at once, and your own involvement in them. Feel the yellow aura envelop you like a blessing, protecting and sustaining you.

Now, visualize the lotus leaves flat on the lake beginning to glow. Gradually, their buds rise up; some remain in germinal state, others begin to open to reveal pink and white pointed petals, and several burst into full bloom. Of these, one is particularly large and beautiful: a giant white flower from which flow effulgent rays of yellow light, like the light you saw before. The central petals are still unfolding, holding you in happy suspense.

Slowly but definitely the petals open to reveal the stamen-like form of a yellow, glowing, ghee-colored goddess standing erect at their center. Gold coins fall in a glittering cascade around her, like a flowing golden curtain.

Lakshmi wears a garland of pink lotus flowers, and her four palms are facing you in blessing. From the lower left of these there falls a steady stream of newly pressed coins of the currency you most use that seem to fall into your lap until you are all but buried in them. Mentally absorb them into your aura; incorporate their weight and color into your astral body until they are no longer visible but you are aware of their presence. Thank Lakshmi for providing you with whatever material means required to fulfill your ambitions.

Her upper left and right hands, meanwhile, hold lotus flowers; these flowers are white and exquisitely scented, and symbolize your transcendence of material attachments. Resolve to use the materials lent to you by the cosmic intelligence to the best of your ability, and to fulfill your own conscience.

In her right lower hand Lakshmi holds a golden pot of amrita, the fluid essence of immortality, health, and life itself. Now, with all the power of your breath and presence, ask Lakshmi to bestow on you ultimate spiritual and physical health and well-being. Even without tasting the bliss juice, you can feel these qualities coming off of her in potent waves. The air is dense as clarified butter but infinitely nourishing.

As the pot comes up, imagine you are swallowing a draught of its sweet liquid contents—something like celestial peach schnapps—and be sure to thank Lakshmi effusively. As you do so, watch the parkland speed itself into a sudden height of summer, one that you know will not be prone to seasonal change. This summer is as permanent as your own fully realized and realizing potential.

Return to your room with the yellow glow still wrapped around you, and light a small yellow, white, or pink candle of thanks to Lakshmi. Place it in a secure position in the window and imagine its rays attracting luck into the house or sit over it for a while welcoming Lakshmi's influence into your life. Envision a part of Lakshmi abiding with you as golden light; in your feet if you wish for luck in real estate issues; in your thighs for wealth; in your genitals for a marital blessing; in your chest if you wish for children or luck on their behalf; in your heart for wish fulfillment; or in your facial features for inspiration and qualities of attraction. Revisit the parkland scene whenever you need a burst of energy, money, or faith.

CHAPTER 5

RADHA

Above all else, Radha loves Krishna. But does Krishna love Radha? Such is the question that taunts her as she goes desolately about her marital duties between illicit meetings. She cares nothing for her status and wealth, or for the shame and destitution that would inevitably ensue should they be discovered; she thinks only of the lowly cowherd in whose company she experiences divine love.

Radha loves Krishna. But Krishna consorts with other women; his attention is divided. Does he too long for her, does he dream of her when he is away? It is agony, the thought of him looking lovingly into the eyes of another… and at the thought of another regarding him as her own, she wants to kill. Immolation at such a time would be a blessing. Rather the searing lick of real fire than exclusion from Krishna's flaming astral aura.

O Stealer of Hearts, the sky is Krishna-blue, the earth is as red as your lips; I cannot breathe without breathing you!

The sight of herself in the mirror sickens her, her beauty wasted. Not for mortal pleasure these perfect limbs, this fathomless gaze. Music that is not his celestial flute insults her ears; all voices that are not Krishna's are like the mindless chattering of apes or the peacock's ugly screech. In Krishna's presence the feathered serpents know to hold their tongues. In Krishna's presence all things are made sacrosanct. Without him, this life is a pointless sham.

All this Krishna knows—yet he still abandons her.

He claims he loves her; he claims she is his ecstasy, and still he goes. Her tears are reciprocated doubled or tripled (Krishna always repays with interest), yet the same day she is alone with her sighs and her clouds and the pain of pretending to be normal.

If her husband knew, he would accuse her… but what does it matter? To Krishna's celestial love song, his words are a mosquito's whine. She must endure the illusion of separation until the cogs of good karma return her to the Krishna-blessed bower.

It does not matter.

Nothing matters, save that Radha loves Krishna, and Krishna loves Radha.

Rahdharani ki jai, Radharani ki jai!

RADHA, SUPREME *GOPI* OR lover of Lord Krishna, is blessed with a love whose fulfillment creates cosmic consciousness and god-realization; yet in some very relatable renditions such as the *Gita Govinda*, she is still prone to the human failings of jealousy and depression. Her relationship also has

Chapter 5

the surprising aspect of being adulterous; surprising, that is, for a religious tract. This incongruity is reconciled when one realizes, as Radha does, that her relationship with Krishna is her life's highest purpose. As such, all obstacles between her and it, whether social, marital, or material, should indeed be hurdled. Her mundane marriage represents the dense material plane, while her interaction with Krishna is a *ras* of cosmic bliss, a dance with divine consciousness in which she must participate at all costs. Radha's dogged persistence parallels that required by the devotee to realize God, and can be applied to all meaningful aspirations. Therefore, an important aspect of Radha's strength is faith in her own conviction, even when this flies in the face of friends, family, and all sensible advice.

Despite the constant reassurances of her cowherd lover—the humble incarnation Krishna has chosen—Radha spends much of the *Gita Govinda* feeling rejected and lovesick. It is her personal quest to fully accept and understand that Krishna's love, metaphorical of God's, is nonexclusive. Likewise, true devotees of the divine seek to gain a unified sense of god-love—a cosmic consciousness in which the ego is dissolved. In Advaita Vedanta (nonduality), the individual is cognizant that "Atman is Brahman"; that is, that every living thing is a part of God, and that God is thus in everything. Oneness with the divine is not so much a goal as a living fact. Radha likewise must learn that she and Krishna are one and can never be apart from one another, or alone: viewed through the light of true spiritual awareness, creation is a whole. Consequently, *viraha*, or love in separation, and unconditional love, are among the gifts that Radha has to offer.

Krishna initiates often seek to emulate Radha's obsessive and all-consuming passion. As Sri Bhaktivedanta Swami Prabhupada, late leader of the worldwide Krishna movement, stated: "The actual perfection of human life lies in always being Krishna conscious and always being aware of Krishna while performing all types of activities." As such, Radha is a shining example of the perfection of yoga. Nothing can tempt her from her devotion. Naturally, this does not apply to everybody's lover, but the element of selflessness and absolute love remains relevant, as of course does the perpetual focus on the divine. Krishna himself represents, and is, pure divine love.

Just as Krishna's flute with its irresistible lure leads lost souls out of delusion and into the light, Radha's example of unconditional love can lead us closer to our divine nature. It might be said that all human relationships are symbolic of our yearning for communion with godhead: there are few more daunting prospects to most of us than being alone in the universe. In sects of two, in familial groups, or in tribes endorsed by the religious or social proclivities of a multitude of others, humankind clings together (often inappropriately) looking for comfort, forgetful of what lies beyond the façade of actions and emotions. Just as Radha sometimes apparently forgot the pure source from which our positive feelings originally sprang, may we also forgive ourselves for forgetting our quest for divine true meaning.

Such thoughts can be socially unconventional (and inconvenient), as is Radha's illicit love for Krishna. Yet the illicitness itself contributes to the strength of their union, as do the long periods of separation during which Radha is grief-stricken. Without the loss, she would not feel the gain so strongly. Unfortunately, this is one of the principles of duality through which this realm functions. Pain exists to heighten pleasure, or so say the wise and experienced. Coping with the day-to-day grievances that no philosophy can salve is one of Radha's functions as a goddess of *prema*, or selfless love for the beloved.

The fifteenth-century poet-saint Mirabai was a devotee of Krishna and a shining example of a latter-day gopi. Despite being born into wealth and status in Rajasthan, Mira gave herself over to the divine madness of transcendental love for Krishna, whom she terms "the Dark One" owing to his blue complexion and the social humbleness that his cowherd avatar represents. In her poem *Ankle Bells* (translated by Robert Bly and Jane Hirshfield), for example, Mirabai declares: "I am at Hari's feet; I give him body and soul/A glimpse of him is water: how thirsty I am for that!"

Water is of course the most holy yet essential of drinks, and the touching of feet the most humble of gestures. She writes elsewhere of drinking the "ambrosial" water that has washed the feet of Krishna, demonstrating the perfection of her bhakti. As author and professor John Stratton Hawley says of the poet: "Her pellucid inner spirituality is contrasted with *samsara*—the cravings and deceptions of the outer world." Like Radha herself, Mirabai

Chapter 5

is divinely obsessed: "The milkmaid has seen his radiant body/And all she can do now is babble." When Krishna is absent, Radha and Mirabai pine, grieve, and fall into a Dark Night of the Soul, for life without divine love is a desert—and worse by far to have tasted that sacred *amrita* and then to be denied it than never to have been blessed, for now these souls know what they are missing! Their union with Krishna is what makes them whole—just as his with them performs the same function. They are actually spiritually symbiotic: just as god manifests as the human individual consciousness that can never be whole until reunited with the original source, both Radha and Krishna are experiencing love through their separation and reunion.

In its most transcendental form, the relationship of Radha and Krishna represents the quest of the Primal Deity to understand its own consciousness, even down to the scariest detail of ego. Another poet-saint of this time who wrote on Radha is Raghunathan das Goswami, who lived many years with Chaitanya Mahaprabhu, spiritual leader and practitioner of bhakti. Of Radha, Raghunathan ruminates: "The ornaments decorating her body are the transcendental ecstasies of love, headed by jubilation/She is garlanded with the flowers of her wondrous virtues, such as her sweet-tongued speech/ She is daubed with perfumed powders that exude from her sometimes sober and sometimes restless moods/Craft and possessiveness are concealed within the braids of her hair."

What does that latter detail bring us, if not the realization that it is possible to be perfect within one's imperfections—"possessiveness" and "craft"—if only these are superseded by union with the divine? Likewise, the *Leelas* or plays and mini-dramas that life creates for all of us exist to teach discernment and to allow spirit to grow through self-realization. We should try to bear in mind that our circumstances, however difficult, tiresome or mundane these may be, are potential living parables offering us what we most need in order to progress spiritually.

There was a time when the last thing women needed was a visualization for selfless love; it was simply a standard requirement of being female. Brothers, husbands, parents, and children automatically came first, and she who did not possess the quality of selflessness to an uncompromising degree was anathema both to herself and to society at large. This is still the case in numerous scenarios. In others, however, "progress" dictates that selfishness in all, including women, is considered a virtue ("you gotta look after number one"), as are materialism and hardened careerism. This single-mindedness has been essential in tipping the balance from rampant chauvinism to a closer proximity to gender equality, but for those of the younger generations brought up with a strong sense of individuality and ambition, indoctrinated that putting oneself first is sensible and right in every situation, it can be difficult to express the gentler traits—the aspects of humanity, not just of femininity, that have been habitually manipulated and recently discarded. This also applies to men, of course, many of whom may not wish to be directed toward materialism and ego. Selfless love, the ultimate strength, may now be perceived as weakness, yet in circumstances not of habit but of conscious choice, and in which one's individual integrity is not threatened, such qualities still have much to offer. This does not necessarily mean being a martyr to a partner, one's children, or an elderly parent in the time-honored manner. The whole point is to act not out of duty but in response to an essentially joyful inner prompting. There are occasions when giving is called for, and when giving is right. There are also occasions when compliance to the demands of others would be mere servility; it is up to one's own intelligence and modernity to discriminate. When it is right, Radha can help us give gracefully by reminding us of the divine harmony of give-and-take, sometimes known as karma.

Selfless spiritual love might be required for either gender when, for example, a partner or close friend needs to broaden their horizons and progress individually—an educational course, an independent trip abroad, a new (or old) social group; such things may make us doubt our position in their affections, inviting into our constitutions the stuttering crone Insecurity, and her shrewish handmaiden, Jealousy. The impact of these vile emotions can only serve to lower one's self-esteem, already shaky in the challenging circumstances. In such situations, it is obvious that the eventual outcome will be of benefit and that the process of individuation is necessary, but selfless love is required to banish these baleful feelings and the fear of compromising one's lifestyle while the loved one pursues the necessary course of action.

It is under these circumstances that Radha will be ready and willing to help, if supplicated. Why go through things alone? There are thousands of deities out there to help bridge the gap between the mortal and the divine. The Queen of Loving Sacrifice, Radha is one among their number who will answer heartfelt calls such as these, given her living and intelligent personality.

Approaching Radha

The first step is to resolve to meet this winsome, passionate goddess and be infused with her capacity for uncompromising love. Radha is an infinitely attractive spiritual being who perfectly combines love with spirituality to the extent that she is supreme amongst Krishna's many adorants and is able to attract he who is himself all-attractive. Radha may be approached, therefore, through the chakras of the heart (green) and the third eye (purple), and as she reigns supreme in the realms of obsessive love, a sense of intense desire and appreciation is helpful in accessing her.

It is beneficial to bathe before any ritual or meditation. Candlelight and essential oils will help create a soft, fragrant ambience appropriate to Radha—try lotus or rose-scented bubbles, or romantic ylang-ylang or jasmine if you prefer essential oils (rose oil can be used but tends to be very subtle in the bath). Salt is not recommended in this particular bathing brew, as it is best to approach Radha honestly. Salt cleanses, but Radha will sympathize with the doubts and insecurities she knows so well.

As always, contemplating, singing and chanting a mantra of the deity concerned is the ideal way to attune. Dance, too, if the mood grabs you. Radha loves to dance.

Letting Go Temporarily: Preparation

This visualization is for those who require a quantity of selfless love to temporarily endure an unwanted compromise. Those who must abandon their desires or relationship altogether should turn to the meditation entitled Cutting the Cords.

As mentioned above, a bath will work wonders for your ability to liaise with this deity.

While in the bath, try to concentrate on the person toward whom you wish to feel selfless love. Consider why you love them, their qualities, and their endearing traits, even those failings that fill you with affectionate amusement.

Try to invoke their Higher Self in your mind's eye—become aware of them as a beautiful, free-flowing spirit with whom you are lucky enough to be involved. Be aware of yourself also as a loving individual with whom this being has chosen to interact for your mutual benefit, not for your mutual constriction.

Contemplate how fortunate you are to have one another in your lives, and the many good things they've done for you. Affirm that the bond between you is strong, eternal, and progressive; your very actions are proving it to be so. At worst, this visualization can only strengthen the love between you. At best, the potential is as limitless as it was when you and your friend, partner, or relative first set eyes on one another.

Visualization for Letting Go Temporarily

Once you have lulled yourself into a loving and appreciative mood, sit on a cushion on the floor or bed, in lotus posture if comfortable, or cross-legged.

First, take three slow, deep breaths.

Now take three more, but as you do so, imagine your body glowing brilliant white. With each inhalation and exhalation, your body's luminosity increases.

With three more slow, deep breaths, envision a stream of electric blue light flowing into the crown of your head and surrounding your body. Feel it penetrating the violet of your third eye zone; see how its color mingles with and intensifies the radiant green of your heart chakra, creating a turquoise area that spreads up and down your body. Feel yourself encapsulated by this vibrating turquoise light.

Listen with your inner ear. Is that a flute being played? Birdsong? Or a peacock's distant squawk?

Visualize a giant lotus flower floating in the air before you. It is shut, but you can tell from the visible petals that it is very pink, a suitable color for a goddess of love. The closed bud gleams with infinite potential.

Now you find yourself at the edge of a lagoon-blue lake, watching the approach of the pink bud nestled in its bed of green. Perhaps you are sitting on a lotus leaf yourself—look down with your inner vision and see. Do not worry if your perceptions are different or even nonexistent; try to feel the approach of Radha, Krishna's favored consort, his shakti, in any way you can.

Everybody has different modes of perception; as the magickal adage asserts, intention is everything.

A low rumble, like distant thunder, provides a continual background to this and many other visions. It is the hum of the universal motor, the sacred syllable *aum* that provides the backbone and is the source of all creation.

Still breathing deeply and slowly, watch as the lotus flower opens. Little by little the petals ruffle outward; in the center, you know the goddess Radha abides.

Compassion permeates the air like sweetly scented pollen in the pink-or-ange sunset; emotions run high and music and poetry are afoot when this deity is present. There is a turquoise sheen on the lotus leaves similar to the color of your own aura; allow yourself to be influenced by the resplendent colors of your vision, just as Radha will respond to her vision of you.

The petals continue to unfurl.

Consider the nature of Radha as you contemplate her emergence from the center of the flower. She too has been forced to let her beloved leave her; mentally make appeal to her compassion. She too has had to transcend personal desire for greater good; offer her the image of your own situation and she will recognize it. She is emerging now, attracted by the familiarity of the plea.

Continue to breathe in and out in blue and turquoise. Allow your spirit to be refreshed by the all-pervading AUM; you feel a thrill of anticipation as the innermost petals gradually reveal the luminous deity.

First you see her resplendent headdress of gold, emerald, and ruby shimmering at the uppermost tip of the center petals. Then Radha's face becomes visible: the blood-red bindi between perfect eyebrows, her enchanting and sympathetic eyes, the golden nose-ring set elaborately with gemstones, her full, smiling lips, and lustrous dark hair flowing down her back. Be aware of her as half-Krishna, just as Krishna is half-Radha. She is indeed his bliss component.

When the goddess has arisen fully in your inner vision surrounding you with a profound sense of beauty and love (if you have "seen" nothing in particular, then this is the thing to look for, the hallmark of Radha's presence), ask her to bestow on you some of her nectar of transcendence. In her slender hand she holds a golden vase; she lifts it toward you.

Mentally explain to the goddess your predicament, which is similar to her own when Krishna had to leave her to fulfill his role as avatar. Request that you, like she, have the faith to gracefully withstand the illusion of separation. Affirm that in this instance, you desire the strength to put another's well-being before your own.

Watch as Radha raises the vase high above your head and baptizes you with the golden liquid it contains. Take the time to fully appreciate the import of this blessing.

Your wish has been granted; Radha will help you in your cause. Connect your third eye with Radha's by envisioning a line of light extending from the middle of your forehead to the center of hers, and feel her sublime acceptance, devotion, and love permeating your aura and falling down your spine in great cleansing waterfalls. You are now bestowed with the strength necessary to surmount any obstacles in the course of your love for the individual concerned.

When you are ready, thank Radha for the wisdom received and return slowly to your position on the floor or bed.

If Radha did not seem to bless you with the heavenly unction, or if you feel a great resistance to your plea—at worst, if all of these visual cues run in reverse in your mind despite your calm state of being—it is time to reconsider your plan of action. Perhaps you have sacrificed your own desires for those of another once too often. Perhaps this level of giving is inappropriate to you in this particular set of circumstances. You cannot force a blessing, and if you fail to receive one, try to accept the higher wisdom inherent in the denial, a wisdom that springs from your inner self and from the goddess petitioned. If a decision is required, try one of the other exercises in the book, such as the weighing-up visualization channeled through Ma'at.

Remember that, in your coming to terms with the situation, it is not just the other party who is being progressed, but you also.

Letting Go Permanently: Cutting the Cords

This is a difficult exercise in anyone's book. If someone we love hurts or abandons us for whatever reason, it can be tempting to turn to Kali for revenge rather than to Radha for loving transcendence, so consider yourself already halfway to moksha if you have chosen this path.

The following visualization is for those who wish to free themselves, as well as the reciprocal party, from a relationship or situation that has become stultified or damaging. When progression along separate paths is painful but necessary, it is time to cut the mundane cords that fetter you both.

Cutting the Cords: Preparation

There are various psychological preparations for this exercise that come naturally to most of us, such as throwing out (or burning) memorabilia, removing obsolete photographs from their frames, possibly rearranging our furniture, adjusting the feng shui, altering the house. If the relationship was that of lover, then new arrangements and color schemes in the bedroom can be particularly effective, as can a cull of lingerie and clothes that remind you poignantly of that person and those times.

However, if you are looking to totally eradicate the wayward party from your psyche, then Radha is not the goddess for you. What she has to offer is not so much amnesia as a positive philosophical appreciation of the past relationship. You can expect a sense of elevation as you realize that the interaction between you and your previous partner or situation was, however disguised, a blessing for both of you. The ability to move forward in the knowledge that you are each fulfilling your personal destinies will then follow. On some levels, you will be more bonded with the person than you were previously, as Radha brings understanding on a soul-level; the most personal of bonds. The mode of interaction will no longer be restrictive or negative, however. Radha is something of a therapy goddess in this sense. Of course, nearly all deities have a healing aspect and may be petitioned as such, but some are more suited to contemporary modes than others. With Radha, faults and failings are accepted and worked with through effort, self-love, and love of others. The cords you will be cutting are not the cords of memory but those of ego-attachment to the person in question. On these grounds, then, may the goddess be approached for this exercise.

A salt bath is recommended prior to this visualization; not because Radha requires us to be purified, but because it can help relieve unnecessary psychic baggage, thus creating a state of grace. As you place the fistful of salt in the water, visualize it glowing blue-white like luminous washing powder, and imagine it having formidable cleansing properties. The grime this substance will be removing, however, is not red wine stains or tricky collar grease, but deeply ingrained astral dirt—that is, the residue of all your negative feelings for and confrontations with the person you are letting go.

As you enter the warm water, watch with your mind's eye as the muck flakes off your body and dissolves. What a relief! By the end of this bath, your aura will be radiant, glowing white, something it has not looked or felt for what seems like ages. You will leave your former tensions, black knots of jealousy, and barbs of spiteful thoughts in the water to be purified by the salt. White candles are recommended to aid this process. A sandalwood or jasmine incense stick will also help put you in the right mood to contact Radha and make this positive step into the future.

Visualization for Cutting the Cords

Settle yourself comfortably, either cross-legged or lying down if you prefer and won't fall asleep. Now take three slow, deep breaths in, hold and out, hold to the count of four each.

Begin the meditation by imagining yourself surrounded by deep blue light. Gradually, it fades hue by hue into brilliant white.

Continue to breathe slowly and deeply; feel the white light streaming through the top of your head, at the crown chakra, and allow some of it to flow out of your solar plexus. You may notice it exiting this region in specific lines like cords—if you glance at their ends you might be able to perceive a specific person or symbol. These are the astral-emotional ties that bind you karmically as well as psychologically to a person. You are looking for those that relate to your ex-partner or the person or situation with which you are splitting. Chances are they will not be hard to find, most likely being the strongest and grubbiest-looking of the lot, though not necessarily. If the situation is painful, they may even look jagged or bloody. Use your intuition to tell you which cords relate to whom.

If you so desire, allow yourself time to study these fascinating relics of your emotional life. This is a good opportunity to throw white light at all of your emotional ties; do so until they look clean and radiant to you, until the unpleasant matter no longer returns.

Now, take a few very deep preparatory breaths in, hold, and out, hold again to the count of four; you are steeling yourself to accept that what you had hoped for has not come to fruition. You must cut the cords for both your sakes. It is not going to be easy, but you are resolved to act in the highest interest of all concerned. You are effectively liberating yourself from a self-chosen bondage.

Holding the bonds you wish to break in your mind's eye, visualize yourself wandering through a forested wilderness in search of the fragrant Radha, in whom you know you will find solace. Now is a good time to let your hurt, grief, and disappointment surface; do not be afraid to feel the sorrow that is natural when saying goodbye to your former dreams.

Seek out Radha among the tangled thickets and shady bowers—you know she's around here somewhere. She will be wearing white, the color of abnegation of earthly values, and her smile will be wiser and sadder than her former dizzy girlish glee. She will probably be glowing like moonlight, with a pearlescent aura broken only by the brilliant red of her bindi. Call to her as you wander the lonely forest.

Continue to breathe the white light, deeply in and deeply out, and remain holding the ties you wish to break; you spot what looks like a silver shadow flitting between two trunks. The trunks are silhouetted, along with their branches, by the light flowing from the fleeting lady. Drawing closer, you perceive the fabulously bright, fawn-like form of Radha.

She will understand your predicament without explanation, but feel free to "state" it if you wish. Perhaps it will help clarify matters in your own mind.

Hold out to her the cords you wish to break.

With your hands extended, proffering the cords unique to you and the person you are letting go, take three extremely deep inhalations and exhalations, while mentally requesting Radharani (Queen Radha) to help you in this cause. Then watch as she raises her silver cleaver and brings it down at your heart, then at your solar plexus. She is so quick and efficient that there is no mess, and the cords snap neatly back into you. Somewhere else, the other person's cords are doing the same thing.

Feel the many new directions you are free to explore. Be aware of the new full scope of your potential. Know that the past can never be taken from you, but the future is all your own. Allow Radha to bestow on you some of her pure silver-white light and bring it back with you when you reenter your earthly space. Breathe the silver in and out and become accustomed to the new sensation of cleanliness and liberation around the bottom of your rib cage. Now that you feel relaxed and refreshed, thank Radha with a flower or some incense, and return to your everyday life, cocooning yourself in Radha's silver aura whenever you need a psychic shower.

If Radha did not respond to your request, there may be more to learn from the situation, even if these lessons are painful. Try to maintain the overview that you hopefully experienced during this exercise, and carry that wisdom back into the situation you feel has become obsolete.

Keep repeating this exercise as needed, or as with all these exercises, improvise accordingly—there may only be a little way to go before you complete this particular experience. When the time is ripe, Radha will come forward to help you continue on your individual path.

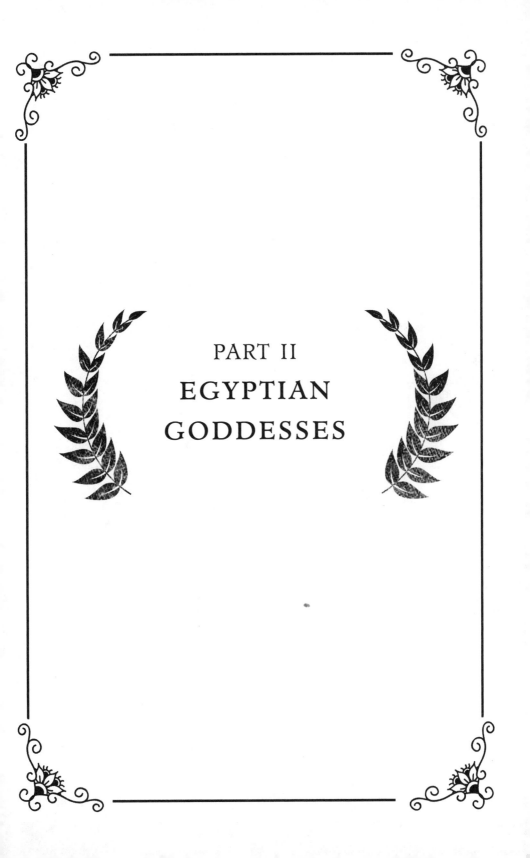

PART II
EGYPTIAN
GODDESSES

CHAPTER 6

ISIS

He was attracted by my soul-greening wings and the moon upon my forehead. He loved my magick; it did not scare him, it entranced. He feared I would bewitch him with my perfumes and my palette of infinite possibilities, but I did not. All that he did, he did of his own free will.

Of course, we knew one another from long ago, for we are soul family; but there can always be new beginnings, new lights in which to behold another. And so we fell in love like two who had never met before, and we were very happy.

Day turned to night in the lover's bower. My moon, so recently so full, cycled around to black. Our shadow-selves began to play, reversing our emotions, deconstructing from the top the patterns we had established.

My other brother, forever jealous, hatched a cunning plan. He had long despised my husband, intent on taking his place and dispatching him to a miserable end. He made a shadow-play to fool my love, to lead him on a merry dance in circles of entrapment.

My husband became confused and fell into a casket of despair, which was soon set adrift on the fast-flowing river, carrying his beloved body far away from me.

I mourned, cut off my hair, refused my food. My magick lost its power because my grief was stronger than my self-belief.

For infinite days and infinite nights I scoured the world for the remnants of my man. I became a kite, soaring high above the homes of happier folk, grief tearing at my heart like a vulture's beak. I could not believe I had allowed a chink in my psychic armor big enough to admit the serpents of destruction. All that I ever wanted had been forfeited by this oversight.

Eventually, I found him. A tree had grown around his body; it seemed that he was made of wood.

I used all that remained of my sorceress's arts to recompose my husband to a semblance of his former glory, but part of him was missing, the part that guaranteed our future together. So, I built him a phallus of wood, and I took his seed through its mediation.

Still deep in grief, I resolved that our offspring should avenge his father's premature demise. Light versus darkness until the dark is conquered, evermore until the karmic debt is paid.

Where do I belong? In between the two; a creature of both. With my companion phantoms I abide between the divine and earthly realms, a contact point for those on either side.

❧

Chapter 6

And I am known by many names: Aset, Great Mother, White Goddess of the Moon; but the name that I prefer is Mercy, for I shall always give it. Through pain and the making of mistakes I have learned compassion. I shall forever remain a willing intercessor and granter of aid to those in need on the stormy seas of life and death alike.

THE WORSHIP OF ISIS, or *Iussaset/Aset* of ancient Egypt, spans thousands of years of active worship. Consequently, she is bestowed with many aspects, each one a reflection of the needs and attitudes of those supplicating her at the time. Isis's functions range from those of a basic goddess of providence, the succoring and fertility-bringing Great Mother, to those of civilizing the people, protecting women and children by engendering marriage and monogamous commitment, and healing with chants, talismans, and medicines.

The original symbolism of her name was that of the throne (later of the pharaoh), and the seat of the soul that is nature. The fertile wonders of the natural world are among Isis's domain. She is often depicted wearing a throne-shaped crown. She also presides over the intellectual complexities of ritual magick. It is unsurprising that for modern metaphysical practitioners, Isis often represents all goddesses from all cultures rolled into one. She is indeed a supreme female deity, her functional scope as wide as her sky-embracing, soul-protecting wingspan.

Isis flew as a kite to find her beloved husband Osiris (*Wesir/Asar*). The writings of Plutarch cohere with those of the Pyramid Texts to provide one of the best-known mythological sagas, of the jealous brother Seth's murder of Osiris and his eventual par-resurrection. Fundamentally a god but living as a man, Osiris was deemed a great civilizing force at a time when barbarism reigned. With the help of Thoth (*Djehuty/Tahuti*), Osiris brought law, agriculture, the alphabet, arithmetic, and philosophical concept to Egypt among many other elevating arts. Leaving the capable Isis to rule in his absence, he issued forth to expand this harmonious civilization as far as Ethiopia, Arabia, and even Europe. Meanwhile, his brother Seth stayed at home seething with envy.

On the return of Osiris, while Isis was away visiting Upper Egypt, Seth and seventy equally disgruntled conspirators threw a welcoming feast for their victorious king… only its aim was to dethrone him for good. Having acquired Osiris's exact measurements and built an exquisite sarcophagus to those specifics, Seth produced the awesome box at the feast, and when much wine had been drunk and the mood was high, he announced that whomsoever it fitted could keep it. Each of the courtiers tried and of course did not win. Finally, Osiris was persuaded to see whether he fitted the coffin: as soon as he lay down, the lid snapped shut. Nails and lead were used to seal it, and the heroic Osiris gasped his last.

Back in Upper Egypt, the terrible news soon reached Isis both intuitively and via her entourage. In abject horror she cut off a lock of her hair and donned the garb of mourning, giving the Greco-Egyptian name Koptos (City of Mourning) to the place at which she learned of her husband's death. Then began a protracted search for his body, which, it was said, had been thrown inside the casket into the Nile. This eventually ran into a tamarind tree (some sources say sycamore) that grew around it and, due to the presence of divinity at its core, produced flowers of unimaginable splendor. The king and queen of the area thus decided to use the tree as a pillar for the palace roof, and promptly had it placed thus, hidden sarcophagus and all.

Isis was joined in her mournful search by her sister Nephthys, who had borne a son by Osiris, the jackal-headed Anubis, but whom Isis in her infinite graciousness had forgiven. Their stalwart search eventually led them to this locale, where sweet-smelling Isis so charmed the people of Queen Athenais that she was invited to the very palace in which her husband's remains were concealed. This palace also housed an infant prince who was terminally ill. Isis, ever compassionate and unrivaled in the healing arts, offered to cure him, so long as she was allowed to do it in her own way.

A very similar myth exists in which the Greek goddess Demeter, this time in search for her daughter Persephone, attempts to cure the son of Queen Meteneira, also demanding trust. Both goddesses place the child in flame, and in both cases, the mother spots this and panics, ruining the process of rendering the child immortal. However, the Egyptian queen recognizes her guest as a goddess, and offers her a gift for her troubles. Naturally, Isis selects the pillar containing the corpse of Osiris, and, having had the sarcophagus removed, she returns the tree to the palace, where it becomes the revered *djed* pillar.

❦

Chapter 6

Using her magick, Isis was able to reanimate Osiris's body long enough to conceive by him. On the Spring Equinox was born to them a son, the falcon-headed *Heru* or Horus, and thus began another saga for the benighted Isis: Seth was of course keen to dispose of this new pretender to the throne. He knew that Horus would grow up to avenge Osiris and wanted to be rid of both father and son. Isis was thus forced into the nomadic life of a beggar, undergoing many trials in order to keep Horus safe from his bloodthirsty uncle, the scorpions of the desert, and other threats to his life. Meanwhile, Seth found the now-embalmed body of Osiris and tore it into fourteen pieces, scattering these far and wide.

Isis rises to this painstaking quest, finding and burying every piece of her husband except for the phallus, which has been eaten by fish. Still Osiris, often depicted with verdure-green skin, represents fertility and provides a basic metaphor for resurrection and for spiritual immortality despite the many trails of the material world. Osiris suffers in the same way that all humans must, even undergoing a shamanic spiritual tearing-apart before he can be re-formed *in perpetua*—yet, like the arrival of the sun, the flooding of the Nile, the shift of the seasons, and the purported resurrection of the pharaoh and mankind itself—Osiris is fundamentally revived. The hard-won legacy lives on: he is the sacrificial solar king who must suffer for his meaningful work and the sake of humankind. This ancient story of course provides an analogy on which several later religious tracts were based. Isis too has solar aspects and is sometimes depicted with a solar headdress. It makes sense that a goddess of agriculture and propagation would include this all-important aspect.

Isis's nurturing qualities are closely allied with those of her sister Hathor. The divine cow is permeated with Isis's presence; cattle are also relevant to Isis in her capacity as civilizer, being facilitators of agriculture and providing both milk and plough-power. Isis is often shown with cow's horns when suckling Horus, and Hathor appears with full cow-visage, resting the young solar god on her knee. This bovine symbolism perfectly exemplifies the perpetual beneficence of motherhood, and both goddesses are depicted wearing cow horns and celestial disk headdress in respect of this.

Another role Isis shares with Hathor is that of "mothering" the pharaoh, the living Horus, and providing him with divine nourishment. Isis, her hieroglyph that of a high-backed throne, was considered quite literally to provide the lap in which the royal backside might place itself. Sitting thus, the pharaoh received both Isis's mother-love and the effects of her wisdom and magick. Consequently, he was invulnerable.

Like many Egyptian deities, Isis is intimately connected with the rising of the Nile and flooding of the Nile valley, until recently so essential to those living in her native country. She is deeply associated with the star Sirius, also known as Sothis or the Dog Star, whose rising heralded (or, it was thought, actually brought about) the inundation of the valley; the growth that ensued is sacred to her. Some believe that her own spiritual genesis occurred somewhere in or beyond Sothis, and that the great Egyptian gods and those of other cultures originated in such starry realms. Arguably, the more that is discovered about the vastness and complexity of the multiverse, and the more one meditates on this and lateral themes, the less implausible such hypotheses become.

On a more terrestrial note, as loyal sister-wife of Osiris and loving mother of Horus, Isis was the obvious deity to whom to appeal in the cause of marital fidelity and the protection of the homestead. She is said to have devised marriage contracts and is protectress of sacred love. It is through Isis that lovers are reunited in new incarnations, particularly those who have undergone a soul-bonding ceremony in their previous lives together.

Isis's vivifying qualities are represented by her ability to become pregnant by the dead body of Osiris and her gathering and subsequent resuscitation of most of his organs. Even when deep in mourning, she motivates herself to action; she does not allow her grief to interfere with the possibility of her love for Osiris becoming his redemption and vengeance, which indeed, through the subsequent forming of their son Horus, it does. She extends this grace to humanity by insisting that Anubis and Thoth invent the art of mummification, and she is sometimes depicted presiding with Ma'at over the process of judgment in the underworld. Isis often wears a vulture headdress, demonstrating her queenly status as well as her connection with the dead body and the recycling thereof, and, importantly, recalling the scattering of her husband's own corpse and its resurrection via air.

❀

The Egyptian *Book of the Dead* describes Isis and her sister Nephthys protecting the soul of the newly deceased from ambush: "O you who are invisible, do not await me, for I am Isis … Isis drives off those that would await me; Nephthys drives off those who would disturb me." Indeed, Isis appears in the Pyramid Texts over eighty times as protector of the "Osiris," here to mean the recently deceased. Her connection with the kite species is attributable to its high-pitched call, similar in pitch to that of a keening mourner.

Isis as healer also nurtures the helpless, crippled aspect of Horus into strength and rectitude, remedying the wrongs done to him by his uncle Seth. Her domestic qualities bring spinning, weaving, and cookery into her domain in addition to healing, sex, and conception. Isis is a perfect goddess to whom to appeal in the cause of stable and spiritual love, as the exercise on finding one's ideal partner indicates.

In addition to her roles as protector and healer, Isis is of course the High Priestess of the Egyptian pantheon, mistress of *heka,* or magick. The form of Isis who wears a solar crown denotes her connection with creative light and her central role in the Egyptian pantheon. By tricking her uncle Ra, once the supreme solar deity, into telling her his names (i.e., the vibrational key to his essence), she procured formidable occult energies for her own use, symbolizing the stage at which the worship of Isis took over from an outmoded priesthood. Her rivalry with Seth tells a tale both spiritual and agricultural; along with his female counterpart Sekhmet, to whom he is married spiritually if not actually (his wife being Nephthys), Seth represents the belligerent, destructive (albeit necessary) aspects of life, while Osiris and Isis represent love and forgiveness. Likewise, with Egypt herself as the metaphor, Isis is the good land, Osiris the fertilizing water, and Sekhmet/Seth the desert. As is now widely recognized, Osiris's myth became integrated into that of another solar deity, Jesus, and Isis's into his mother, Mary: of course, both *pietàs* end in the salvation of light via resurrection.

Isis is also a goddess who opens the inner eye, revealing the mythos behind the veil of delusional mundanity. A fascinating example and partial explanation of this process on an interpersonal level is given in Dion Fortune's classic novels *Moon Magic* and its prequel *The Sea Priestess*, both of which are highly recommended. The fictional format stirs the imaginative faculty, doorway to many magicks, which is precisely why each chapter of this very book begins with a creative passage on the relevant goddess. The author is thus allowed to seamlessly impart knowledge both symbolic and factual. Times have certainly changed, but the principles concerned remain both entertaining and relevant.

Isis may be spotted wearing the sun disc, but she is primarily a lunar deity, counterpart to solar Osiris, who, owing to his propensity to move below the horizon after sunset, rules additionally over the underworld. Isis knows the secrets of the dead and living alike; she understands the obsessions and fantasies of the individual soul, or *ka*; she is the Guardian of Dreams. She is said to unite with humans as they sleep, bestowing the healing energies and life-giving light required for sustenance. By sleeping in Isis's temple, devotees hoped to gain guidance and help in dreams. This is the shadow-side of her role as mother and nurturer, protector of women and marriages. She epitomizes feminine mystique, beauty, and quiet power. With her exquisitely braided dark hair, heavily kohled eyes, lunar disk headdress, and heavenly perfume, Isis presents a striking figure, but psychologically hers is the art of understatement and subtlety—she is almost always taciturn.

Isis's gifts do not come cheap. She will demand a sacrifice, and it may be something very dear to her prospective devotee—their social life, a source of spiritually unhelpful pleasure, a beloved partner whose presence is not conducive to her plans, or simply one's complacency. Isis can be as harsh as she is mysterious, but her rewards are indubitable. Such is the process of magickal initiation.

Isis presides over the tides of the ocean and its unplumbed depths, symbolic of the subconscious, and, therefore, over other lunar-influenced systems such as the menstrual cycle. Many plants have specific lunar correspondences—rosemary, for example—and these are amongst the most sacred to her, especially the medicinal.

Clearly Isis is a goddess of numerous facets who can be appealed to on a vast array of topics. Her temple in Philae bears a plaque summarizing her superlatively cosmic nature: "I separated earth from heaven, I showed the path of the stars, I regulated the course of the sun and the moon." It is on the great magickal and spiritual aspects of Isis we shall focus in the following exercises.

Encountering Isis: Preparation

Owing to her cosmic nature, whichever time feels right to you will be good for accessing Isis. Traditionally the evening of a full moon, at twilight, or any crepuscular period such as dusk or very early dawn will do, the former being preferable. This is even better by the sea on the night of a full, clear moon, or if you can't manage outside, in your makeshift temple nearing midnight. In all cases, the contact is enhanced by feeling excited, moody, menstrual, or highly strung, so don't worry about those apparent drawbacks if you have them. They can be helpful in attracting the cosmic healers.

A little pomp and ceremony will befit you to encounter this ultimate mistress of ritual magick. For example, you could wear a special cloak or silver headdress perhaps featuring a moonstone and invoke the quarters and cast a circle prior to the visualization. Covenesque paraphernalia (chalices, athames or ritual daggers, statues of the god and goddess, for example) may help reconfirm your rapport with the goddess; however, these are psychological props and not necessities. As with the preparations for all of the visualizations, use and do what feels right to you.

Burning a little rosemary or myrrh, or using jasmine, sandalwood, or lotus while you meditate or in your bath will help you get on the Isian wavelength. An aromatic, candlelit soak with a little salt in the water for purification will help prior to the visualizations.

For channeling the intuitive, psychic aspect of Isis—her priestess self as it were—a lunar bath prior to the visualization will be helpful. You may leave moonstones (if you have some) and a little salt in cold water for thirty minutes (or longer) and add to the bathwater, or to a washcloth if you don't have a tub; this will endow it with the vibrational qualities of this gem. A little almond milk can be added, and you can gather mother of pearl and silvery objects on the side of the bath to admire by candlelight as you soak. Isis or moon incense with rosemary overtones will naturally be of benefit. Candles can be white, royal blue, purple, or black.

Envision the bath glowing with silvery pearlescent light. As you step into it, feel yourself entering the liminal zones between worlds; a place inhabited by beings conversant in the material and spiritual worlds alike. Feel the realities mixing, the similarity between shadows and solids, dog and wolf, the living and the dead. Watch their half-recognized forms move about the room as you lie in the warm water. This is the real twilight zone, right here in your bathroom.

If you have some purple solarized water (see the introduction), add it to the moon water when you have mentally established its lunar properties. As you do so, imagine the bath flooding with purple light and energizing the purple of your third eye area. Watch it glow until it illuminates the room. Be aware of stepping into silvery-purple water as you enter the bath.

As you soak, center your energy on your forehead, in the area above the bridge of the nose, and between the eyebrows. Purify yourself for as long as you need and imagine the white light of the salt in the water dissolving all unwanted negative feelings and any mundane fatigue and preoccupations you may be harboring. Enjoy the shapes of the steam and incense as well as the shadows thrown by the objects in the candlelight. Let your imagination loose as you lie in your vibrant bath.

When finally you emerge, see your body glowing pearly white, with a brilliant purple forehead.

You are now prepared for a powerful goddess visualization.

Visualization for Increased Powers of Intuition

Sit comfortably before a white or purple or sea-colored candle, at twilight if possible. To make sure the candle doesn't blow out when you exhale, place it in a glass lantern or at a distance.

Take several deep, slow breaths, and hold the air in your lungs for five seconds at a time; wait five seconds before you inhale again. As you do so, you are charging your astral body up for flight, and making yourself more visible to the great goddess Isis. Imagine your body glowing brighter with every breath and feel the new pranic energy tingling in your body. Don't forget to keep the third eye area drenched in purple light.

Now visualize the silver orb of Isis's headdress. Notice the special quality of the astral silver, so pure that it can pass effortlessly between dimensions. Draw back a little to admire the crescent moon boat beneath it. Is it on her forehead or not? It is difficult to tell. Now that you look a little closer, it almost seems to be painted onto cloth...

Moving back, the full figure comes into view: Isis kneeling, her wings outstretched, her face set in an enigmatic smile; a picture on a veil. Behind it, you know the goddess abides, but you will have to penetrate the veil to find her.

Taking a few more pranic breaths, resolve to acquire the energy to find her, wherever she might be. You need to increase your powers of intuition and realign your mundane self with your Higher Self, and who better to guide you in this than the mistress of magick herself? Call to Isis as you begin to mentally move through the veil. Imagine yourself being propelled forward as you do so. Use your willpower to pass between realities.

Behind the veil, you find water. It is black and white; an ocean at night. The darkness of the water meets the darkness of the sky, and both are eternally deep; the water's surface is delineated by the flashing of silver wavelets far beneath you. You are traveling very fast, in lotus posture, between the deep, dark sea and the blue-black sky in which a single silver orb is hanging.

Eventually you see a vast throne of white marble rising out of the water. A pillar stands on both sides of the throne, the left one black and the right white, and seated at its center is the glowingly visible, slender form of a veiled woman.

As you approach, you are endowed with a strong sensation of vibrancy and awe. You travel toward her sandaled feet, and prostrate yourself at the feet of the goddess, mentally making your plea.

She tells you to arise, and you hover before this larger-than-life white-clad figure, admiring the fluidity of her form, suggestively concealed, at once ancient and youthful. You will doubtless have personal impressions at this point that cannot be predicted. Try to memorize as much as you can for further analysis and use.

Still, you have not seen the face; just a teasing hint of black hair at the edges of the veil. Just as you are wondering how to glimpse behind it, Isis raises her right hand and taps you sharply on the forehead between the eyebrows.

As Isis touches your third eye, you receive an image of import. A message is delivered in the goddess's resonant voice. Listen carefully to the words chosen, however bizarre they may seem, and write them down, along with any other impressions you receive, or, if you do not wish to break your concentration by making notes now, be sure to memorize what is said, and record it as soon as you emerge from your meditation.

You may receive confirmation of your life path or a cryptic criticism; you may receive a clue to your future, or advice about your progression. Whatever is said, do not forget that your purpose is to increase your intuitive capacity, so let it be known that this is the purpose of your visit. You may also be told whether you will ever penetrate the veils.

If the response is positive, continue your internal dialogue for as long as you feel inclined. Once you have established a rapport with Isis on this fundamental level, it will be easier to access her at any time of day or night and to slip into the part of your personality that allows you to contact higher intelligences. And of course, the more you practice and enhance your intuition and inner vision, the stronger they will become.

In the case that you received nothing or a negative image, return to your physical space. An interest in psychic studies is inappropriate to you at this point in time.

Visualization for Magickal Ability

Magickal ability is the art of directed will combined with strong spiritual integrity, visualization and emotion, sometimes aided by props both psychological and physical. Therefore, the best way to increase it is to practice both virtues—kindness, abstinence, generosity—as well as concentration techniques. It goes without saying that yogic, mantric meditation is ideal for developing focus and spiritual attunement. Alternatively, you could think of something that provokes a strong inner reaction for this exercise, perhaps something you really long for, and try formulating your feelings into a golden net and "capturing" it. However, if you prefer something more ritualistic, this may be the visualization for you.

Arise from your ritual bath empowered but in the humble knowledge that you are a mere neophyte (no matter how far you have come down the magickal path) to the supreme High Priestess you are about to encounter. You know you have a long way to go, but you are confident of your ability to achieve formidable occult prowess. This is partly because you know you are prepared to put in the effort.

Take several deep breaths; envision yourself breathing in light as you do so. Feel the light penetrating every cell of your physical body and every atom of your astral one. Flex your psychic muscles by extending your aura to the periphery of the room, making it glow as brightly as you can, and then withdrawing it again.

Now, stimulate your chakras one by one; concentrate on each in turn, starting at the base chakra. Make the red discus spin and, as it does, feel yourself attuned to your primal self. Then work your way up the orange intestinal area, the yellow solar plexus, the green heart, the blue of the throat, and the purple pineal chakra. Finally, as you concentrate on the golden-white discus at the top of your head, feel yourself assimilating the cosmic energy that infiltrates all aspects of being.

Now that you have limbered up, imagine yourself flying at high speed through astral space. You may see anything at this point; landscapes, strange geometric shapes, symbols—it's down to your own intuition and inner vision.

Whatever you see, feel the sensation of flying. Hear the whirring of your chakras—AAAUUUMMMMMM—like propellers driving you forward. Keep your ultimate goal in your mind's eye: a deity who embodies magickal ability and in whose very presence your own aura and ability will rise to new heights.

Eventually you reach the throne. It sits at the water's edge like that of the tarot's Queen of Cups, and on both sides is a pillar, the left black and the right white. There are offerings on the steps before it: pomegranates, votive candles, and mummified animals, mainly ibises and cats.

The Priestess is unveiled and very beautiful in the moonlight. Her heavily kohled eyes assess you with an air of nonchalance.

Now it is up to you to prove your worth. Shine as brightly as you can; present your soul and your will to learn the magickal craft and see if she accepts it. Watch her hands. A small gesture may indicate acceptance or rejection. (If she appears to reject you, return to your room and resolve to practice until you reach an acceptable level. Or, it may be the wrong time in your life for such endeavors; be sure to interpret the response in the light of your personal circumstances and be as realistic as possible about it. Only you will know what the real cause is.)

Isis

If the Isis figure bids you proceed, move forward with quiet humility and bright aspiration. Mentally communicate to her the object of your quest and be sure to add (and feel) that you will use your abilities to the greater good of humanity. There is no point in applying to Isis if your ultimate aim is selfish, manipulative, or harmful power; she, like most godforms, is unwilling to co-operate with plaintiffs such as these. If the aim is self-development, healing arts, or spiritual progression, however, she is likely to respond favorably.

Now that you are in Isis's presence, see how she reacts to you. She may touch some part of your astral body, which indicates the need to develop it, or she may even bestow instant healing; she might shape-shift and take you on a journey. Whatever it is, go with it for as long as you feel confident. The Wiccan adage "perfect love and perfect trust" is particularly applicable to Isis. She will reward those who put their entire faith in her; do not forget, she is nature. Like Kali in her most fearful aspect, she will never betray those who deliver themselves unquestioningly into her hands, though as a final test of faith, she may produce the illusion of doing so.

Make sure you request, plainly and clearly, the augmentation of the psychic powers you already possess. Compare yourself to Isis prior to her empowerment and confirm that you too will use your abilities in a positive manner. As you depart Isis's domain, she may hand you a package or talisman. Be sure to keep a hold of it and feel it in your hands on your return.

It is difficult to describe this astral-internal trip as it will be very different in the case of each individual. Whatever you experience, stay with it until you feel inwardly fulfilled, and when you return to the room, consciously bring your new power with you. Much of it may be in the form of confidence and resolve.

You are now ready to write down and interpret the experiences you have just had, possibly in a Book of Shadows. The symbolic aspects of your visualization are likely to be important signposts to you on the magickal path.

Visualization for Finding Your Ideal Long-Term Partner(s): Preparation

Note: As with all exercises, the state of mind induced in this visualization is used to facilitate a particular archetypal response and does not represent the author's personal opinion regarding celibacy or any other lifestyle. Also, with the recent popular rise of polyamory, and the author herself knowing several happy gay, trans, and bisexual combined triumvirates/partnerships, please adapt to your own specifications.

This visualization is best performed when you have tried the conventional methods of attaining a suitable counterpart and are feeling disappointed and even depressed by your apparent inability to do so. Consequently, it is intended for those who are single rather than those who are in a relationship, though of course it is up to the reader's discretion whether they perform it when already involved. However, the intent should not be to turn a particular person into your long-term partner. The idea is to attract to you a person who already harbors the specific qualities you seek rather than altering or compromising another's personality.

Before charging into a long-term situation, it might be worth remembering that life experience is an essential ingredient to almost any relationship these days, particularly if it is to have a spiritual dimension; long gone are the days of marrying the first person who comes along, premature monogamy and subsequent self-stultification in the name of partnership. However, if a younger person finds themselves attracted to this visualization, it may be right for them at the time. It must be acknowledged that some souls are older than others, and experience cannot be represented by an annually changing number. Use your integrity to decide whether a visualization with such permanent repercussions is really what you want, no matter how old or young you might be.

If you feel somewhat battered and bruised by life; if you've really been there and done that and have had it up to the back teeth with learning processes and formative experiences and being a one-person band, then this exercise could help answer your prayers.

If possible, the following preparations should be performed at twilight on the night of a waxing or full moon, with the visualization following directly afterwards. For a magickal visualization of this nature, it is helpful to pamper yourself prior to the exercise.

Take a long hot candlelit bath with an herbal infusion; add a few drops of fragrant essential oil such as rose or geranium. Bubbles in the bath are

Isis

appropriate both to Aphrodite, whose properties are relevant to your cause, and to *Isis Pelagia*, the Lady of the Waves. This is an oceanic aspect of Isis you will be dipping into later. If you like, treat yourself to a glass of wine (or the drink of your preference) while in the bath, and listen to some music that makes you think of the sort of person you would like to have as a partner.

Allow yourself to daydream about your ideal partner—how they might look, how they will treat you, the type of conversations you will enjoy together. If you want to share children or animals, imagine them too. Try to get as accurate an image as possible of what you want from your future without imagining any one person in particular.

Observe the shadows that flicker around the bathroom as you lie swathed in steam. These may seem insubstantial, but they are created by solids. Your imaginings are also a real reflection of your future, which can be crafted into anything you want. Resolve to create your own reality in the style of your choosing. The materials are out there. All you need to do is home in on them.

Arise from the bath when you feel attractive and confident; perform your toilette as if you were about to meet the partner of your dreams. When you smell and look gorgeous, retire to the room in which you plan to perform the visualization.

Visualization for Finding Your Long-Term Partner(s)

Light three small candles of green, blue, and white, respectively. As you light them, be aware of the flames as a focus on the astral plane, attracting the type of person you wish for.

Take several deep breaths of light, in and out, but hold the light in your body, and resolve to enhance your partner's or partners' energies by investing your own willpower into the flames, whose light crosses the dimensions and sends a clear signal into the emotional worlds. Sit comfortably before them and envision yourself flying through the air, very fast over the twilit trees and houses, then over the fields that lead to the sea.

Notice the full moon, hanging huge and low in the sky, a surreal white-silver orb imprinted with the face of the goddess. Tell her your woes as you travel toward the ocean. Do not be afraid to have a good moan; you've been through the mill on this simple quest, and for what? It is not that much to ask—a decent partner and a happy home life—is it? Why can't it all be as straightforward as this flight?

As you journey toward the silver and black ocean's edge, you grow more and more depressed about your lot. The black of the sea and sky seems to reflect your mood, and the cliff tops you are rapidly approaching look like the edge of the world, the land's very end.

You come to a halt at the cliffs and gently descend over them into the frothing white foam at the black ocean's edge. The water is very deep and probably quite perilous, but you don't care. Without that craved-for company, what is there to live for anyway?

In your despair, the water begins to look quite inviting. You put one foot in, and a wave instantly engulfs you. You struggle to the surface, but another one is on you now. Seven times you rise gasping to the surface, and seven times you are submerged in the black salt water.

Exhausted, you focus on the full moon hanging over the water and address Isis, Queen of Heaven.

At this point, project the images you had whilst preparing, of your ideal types and the life you would share together, and mentally compare them to your current circumstances. Ask Isis to work on your behalf, to lift you from your misery and grant you what you know to be simple and possible.

Address her as Queen of All Women and Initiator of Marriage Contracts; if relevant, appeal to her as Patroness of Parital Fidelity and Family Life. Tell her that you feel you have lost your Osiris—or Nephthys—she will understand your yearning. Appeal to her as a soul who knows how it feels to be bereft of one's complementary aspects.

Now watch as Isis arises from the sea. She is vast and impossibly beautiful; her eyes are veiled but perceptibly shining with compassion. Twin serpents entwine on her headdress; between them is a silver crescent moon. A merciful smile plays about her ravishingly red lips; in her hand she bears aloft a cornucopia.

Around her waist she wears a knotted girdle. If you wish to have children in the future, the powers of this girdle are of particular relevance to you. You could appeal to the Great Enchantress with this aim in mind.

As with most of these visualizations, you are likely to have personal experiences that are impossible to predict here. Spend as much time as you need with Isis, letting your emotions go, purging any negative hang-ups you may have from previous experiences. Be sure to stay by the water's edge in the moonlight until you are feeling positive and strong. Above all, do not forget to continually request the granting of your wish for an ideal partner.

When you have very strongly projected your previous daydreams in the direction of Isis's forehead, along with your request for their coming to pass in the material world, and are feeling confident and uplifted, you are ready to return. Thank the goddess for her help and promise to do your very best by what is granted to you as a result.

Fly back over the fields, houses and roads until you reach the window of your room. See yourself sitting before the candles and reenter your body.

Open your eyes safe in the knowledge that everything has been done to bring about your heart's desire. Every time you look at the moon, you will strengthen the spell. Every time you think of the ocean, you will be reconfirming your purity and ability to move on emotionally.

Try to feel as if you have met that person already, as if you are already in love, perhaps recalling other situations or even incarnations in which you were in such a relationship. Tuning in to cosmic love itself will obviously also be of great benefit. With the "in love" aura wrapped around you, full of gratitude and generosity, you will obviously prove extra attractive to everyone, including your future partner(s). Be aware that you are drawing them to you with the strength and confidence of your belief and are consequently making your own reality.

Having created this magickal atmosphere, you can have a lot of fun simply observing who comes into your life at this point and the situations that arise. As all such circumstances are metaphorical of inner truth, you can learn a great deal by analyzing and interpreting them.

Most importantly, enjoy yourself. You have done your best to attract your complementary other(s), and fate may be encouraged but certainly cannot be forced. The most conducive thing you can do at this juncture is remain happy and relaxed.

Now, let nature take her course.

❧

Chapter 6

CHAPTER 7

NEPHTHYS

In the nebulous light of the eventide she loses herself once again to the realms of imagination.

She sees herself as she might have been, as she might yet be: a queen among women, lady of the house, her beautifully decorated palace swarming with congratulatory consorts. Her future sons.

Isis will arrive soon, freeing her from the grim reality of her circumstance. Together they will fly to Isis's home, bright with tapestries and fragrant with herbs, to play with the infant Horus, who grows stronger and more golden by the day. Of course, this house will be the first to suffer when he reaches maturity; but Isis will see her right.

About her husband Seth, she does not care. She blames him for her unfulfilling spectral life, her sense of limbo.

She welcomes these uncertain lights, concealing shades, the times when nothing can be done. It is the working hours she hates, the bright focus on her inaction, the temptation to feel pointless and guilty. There must be more to it than this.

Small things distract her. She paints, she scribes vivid glyphs. Sullen but tinged with hope, she waits.

What is Isis doing now? Not only can she embalm herself with the memories of a thousand nights with Osiris, brightest of the gods, but she has the best magick, the best infant, the most illuminating shadow-sister in the worlds.

If her own life is a void, she can at least use it to throw Isis into relief. Vicarious fame is not such a bad thing; better than infamy, she considers.

Taking heart, she lights the lamp and awaits her beautiful friend and sister. They are made of the same soul-substance, indubitably. The evening star is risen; soon Isis as the morning star will bring her dawn.

And then will they be balanced and inseparable; infinitely bound by spice-pungent funerary tresses of immortal experience.

NEPHTHYS (NEBET-HET) IS ISIS'S sister and Seth's wife, and one of the Great Ennead of Heliopolis. Married to the God of the Desert, she is unable to conceive by him, establishing her position as deity of the unmanifest whereas Isis is Goddess of Fertility and Growth. However, Nephthys is unhappy with this role and determines to become pregnant by Osiris. Consequently, she disguises herself as Isis and seduces her sister's husband. By this act of deception, she conceives Anubis, the jackal-headed God of Divination.

Shortly thereafter, Seth succeeds in dispatching his hated brother Osiris to an untimely end in a casket on the Nile. Isis, wild with grief, is approached by her guilty sister, who fears for the life of her unborn child. Isis, ever merciful, helps Nephthys hide Anubis in the underworld, and together the two sisters seek Osiris. Thus, Nephthys is accomplice to Isis and fellow healer and resuscitator of the murdered king.

In many respects, Nephthys is Isis's shadow, echoing and underlining the roles of her sister goddess as protector and healer. Together they create one of the dyads so popular in ancient Egypt as a reflection of widely held belief in the duality of nature and in the binary aspect of ultimate reality. On coffins and in depictions of Rites of the Dead, Nephthys appears opposite Isis mourning over the body of the deceased, the "Osiris" of the situation, while casting her expansive wings over them in protection. Likewise did she mourn with Isis over their lost-and-found lover, sometimes taking the form of a kite in her grief. She is appealed to in conjunction with Isis to protect and guide the dead, but while Isis is explicit and manifest, Nephthys is implicit and invisible. Yet she helps maintain the Ennead and supports their good works from a liminal position: she often wears a pillar headdress denoting her role as "Lady of the House," one meaning of her name. Pillars support a roof but are not usually appreciated in their own right.

Though married to a god of plight—yet one necessarily so and arguably misunderstood—Nephthys bears him no allegiance. Indeed, most of her actions attempt to rectify what the hand of Seth has spoiled. She complements Isis's role by counterbalancing it; where Isis is the dawn, Nephthys is dusk; where Isis is the new moon, Nephthys is the old; where Isis is fecund, Nephthys is menstrual: the pharaoh himself was said to be composed of her magickal fluid.

Often, the two goddesses are barely distinguishable from one another. Nephthys cleaves to her powerful sister's side, shape-shifting to avoid her own belligerent husband and aiding and abetting Isis in her perpetual fight against turmoil. She is therefore a suitable deity to approach for the purpose of putting wrongs to right. She is an especially apt accomplice when a faulty judgment or an error on our part has led to a rift in a friendship; perhaps trust has been betrayed or a relationship vilified. If you feel you have committed a wrongful action and wish to put it right, the following visualization should help.

Visualization for Making Amends

A good time to approach Nephthys is at twilight on a night of a dark moon.

First, think as honestly as you can of the traits you dislike about yourself and that you feel have caused the current situation. Imagine them encapsulated in a black sarcophagus.

Now envision yourself in your most positive light, glowing with all the good qualities you know you also possess. This image too takes the form of a sarcophagus, but this time it is golden. The two figures molded from your essence seem to be taking on a life of their own. You see them standing side by side on the bank of a swift-flowing river, slowly becoming animate.

The black sarcophagus, now more of a living corpse, turns toward your golden self and pushes it into the river. Very quickly it is borne downstream.

You have a choice: you can either stand by and witness all your virtues being wasted, allowing yourself to be taken over by your own darkness, or you can try to redeem the situation.

Call upon Nephthys, sister of Isis and her fellow healer, to help you now. Watch as she appears above you, a beautiful bird with a wingspan so vast that it seems like the sky itself. Will her to descend.

When Nephthys has landed, attach yourself to her by envisioning a line of light between your third eye and hers, and ask her to help you find your qualities again.

Nephthys lifts you up and bears you over the bright ribbon of river until you spot your golden body bobbing up and down below. Descend and re-claim it. As it clambers on board, re-assimilate it into your soul.

The task is not over yet, however. There is still the black sarcophagus, container of all the traits you despise in yourself, to deal with.

Nephthys returns you to the starting point. Elevated above your negative self, you feel liberated, freed of trivial concerns, petty jealousies, and all other emotions that exacerbated the situation in the first place. Your negativity, once so powerful, looks faint and feeble from up here.

As you realize this, Nephthys swoops down and bears you within arm's length of the black container. Use all your strength and determination to shove or kick it into the water.

Chapter 7

The sarcophagus opens with the impact, and the black body it contains begins to unravel. Funerary bandages, known in old times as "tresses of Nephthys," fan out in the water like matted strands of filthy hair undergoing a long-required wash, or so it seems from your newly regained aerial vantage point.

As the past is borne away, you feel a tremendous weight being lifted from you. The water is fast and soon inundates the splitting sarcophagus, purifying and transforming its putrid contents. They are being scattered on the currents, turned to silt and rubble. Before very long, there is nothing left to see.

Silently, Nephthys glides to the ground and allows you to dismount. Your aura is shining with a golden luster and you feel relaxed and happy.

Breathe in and out deeply, expanding and enhancing this golden aura until Nephthys departs. She will only leave you when you are mended.

If you have hurt someone else in the situation you are healing, send them your heartfelt apology on a tide of this golden energy. Convey all of your will to heal them—all the love and affection you have ever amassed for them as fellow travelers on the earth plane. Keep pouring this healing light from yourself into them until you really feel them absorbing it at the other end.

Once you have finished, if possible, try to make amends on the physical plane too. If your apology is not accepted, try not to get angry or allow negative energies just when you have freed yourself of them.

While talking or writing to the person concerned, keep visualizing this vivid golden light of cosmic forgiveness. You are able to forgive them because you have blessed yourself with forgiveness also, and because ultimately you are both part of the cosmic whole: we are in fact all one another and all living things. Because you know how difficult it can be to really feel this and to be empathetic, how easy it is to be swept away by the strong currents of emotion, you are able to be lenient about the transgressions of others.

When you are ready, thank Nephthys and repeat the exercise whenever you feel the unworthy side of your nature taking control. Try to maintain the golden, light-filled self at all times. Send the dark thoughts downstream, particularly when they threaten to interfere with a friendship or relationship again. It is not worth giving into them, for emotion is fleeting while repercussions can resound through the ages. Make amends before it is too late.

Nephthys

CHAPTER 8

HATHOR

Hathor shakes her sistrum to chase away bad spirits; here, everything is safe. It is a walled garden, a sanctuary from evil. Children play insulated from harm, enfolded in her motherly love. Ribbons of scent unravel on the breeze: flowers and honey, freshly baked cakes, and rich dairy foods promise pleasure in futurity.

Hathor rattles her silvery sistrum and creates rhythmic music the small children dance to.

Her heavy cow's head, long-lashed and smooth of line, nods in mild approval of the scene. Brown eyes reflect no sentiment, just a simple natural warmth and the will to gently protect. Her expression is opaque as milk, pure mystery of the mother-goddess.

The red-brown earth is rich as cake, and even difficulties here are made palatable. Hathor has designed her domain to delight. Plants and vegetables of all shades of green flow from their carefully nurtured furrows and beds, and they are graced by flowers and butterflies of entrancing color.

Frothy orchard trees grow at the base of one giant sacred sycamore—Lady Hathor's den. Here she comes to consider those from whom life has been taken; here she brings foodstuffs and gifts for the untimely dead.

Nobody who supplicates Hathor will go without; she makes it a point of honor to give whenever asked. Beauty belongs to her, and it is her will to share it. In return, she asks only that her protégés be equally generous of self and that they too offer practical help to those in need. Need is anathema to Hathor: she would eradicate it if only the gods would permit.

Her rivals continually evoke imbalanced desire in humankind to tip the scales of Ma'at that she keenly observes. Still, Hathor and her kind will give and suckle and fortify and cushion and nurture until it is proven that the milk of kindness can never run dry. Milk is a better substance than blood, at least in Lady Hathor's spellbook; blood can augur death while milk means life. Thus, she hopes to prove her loving point.

HATHOR IS ONE OF the oldest Egyptian deities; she is sometimes represented as a woman wearing the horns of a cow on her head between which rests a solar disc, or else she has cow's ears. However, she is more often to be found as a chimera goddess with the body of a human female and the entire head and neck of a cow. Cattle were revered in ancient Egypt for the same reason they are sacred in Hindu belief—their unquestioning beneficence. They provide their young and thereby us too with milk, the most obvious symbol of motherhood; they aid agricultural labor, fertilize the earth with their manure, and their providence seems unconditional like a mother's love.

Hathor presides over conception and childbirth and is primarily a goddess of women. In the Coffin Texts of the Middle Kingdom, Hathor is called Great Mother, the Primeval, the Lady of All, and is said to live on Truth or Ma'at. Although many deities such as Nut, Isis, and even Sekhmet are attributed this archetypal role at times, her connection with Ra's epoch of power, her solar disk headdress, and her night-sky-colored skin in early depictions suggest Hathor's greater antiquity as such. She is Patroness of the Pharaoh and was considered to sustain him with her divine nourishment, just as she suckled Horus in his infancy. In accessing the Hathor within, we can tap into the eternally compassionate and unquestioningly loyal side of our natures, particularly into divine maternal love.

Another name for Hathor is "Mother of Light," an appellation that underlines her life-giving properties. It was she who gave the souls of the dead the sustenance they required beyond the grave, so that they might live on and eventually return to be reborn. She wears a *menat* necklace symbolizing this regeneration. As a counsel of seven cows, Hathor determined the incarnational lessons of each soul and the circumstances required to facilitate them. She often appears as the Lady of the Sycamore Tree; this tree is said to have surrounded the body of Osiris when it was eventually washed ashore (in other versions it is tamarind). Many Egyptian coffins were made of sycamore in respect of this connection, a wood associated through Hathor and Isis with the properties of resurrection.

In the typical Egyptian manner, Hathor is both the daughter and wife of Ra, the supreme solar deity and master of magick until Isis supplanted him. Together they produce an aspect of Horus symbolized by the rising and setting of the sun: his diurnal regeneration. In other texts, Hathor is the wife of Horus, his parentage being of Isis and Osiris. As the son of the latter, other traits of Horus are emphasized, of personality and spiritual development. Hathor is connected with the physical dimension of the god and mistress of growth and its limits.

Just as the pharaoh became the living Horus, the queen became an incarnation of Hathor. Again, she functions as both his mother and his lover. It

Hathor

has been conjectured that in performing both of these roles, Hathor symbolically transcends all sexuality; conversely, it cannot be ignored that Egyptian mythology (and its history) is replete with incestuous relationships.

A much fiercer aspect of this generally benevolent goddess is her transformation into Sekhmet. Mythologically speaking, Hathor becomes the "Eye of Ra" and watches the transgressions of mortals from a solar vantage point. When roused by their vile behavior and their insulting of the gods, particularly of Ra, whom they call "old," she transforms into Sekhmet, the bloodthirsty lioness whose wrath and bloodlust is so great that her feet become red from wading in the blood of the enemies of Divine Order. This is highly reminiscent of gentle Parvati's transformation into Kali. Once her ire is roused, Hathor-Sekhmet can only be assuaged by trickery—alcohol colored red to resemble blood, which she thus drinks and falls asleep, thereby curtailing her slaughter. For his part, Ra is shocked that he has been unable to control his own kin, indicating his perceived decrepitude and outmoded rule at this point in Egyptian history.

The deities Hathor and Sekhmet may seem distinct and separate today, but their previous interplay reflects how deep still waters can run ... and how far a tranquil personality can go when pushed. The divine Hathor is, however, an antithesis of Sekhmet: the ancient Egyptians were famously dualistic in stance. (For more on this, see for example the relationship between Isis and Nephthys.)

Hathor's personal history is conversely devoid of complexity; though she may be coupled with other goddesses such as Nut and Isis, as an individual deity she exudes simplicity. She is, one could almost say, the fact of life, as well as its sustainer. She presides over love, music, joy, creativity and the harmonious domicile. As a deity to whom to appeal, she is eminently suited to long-term projects and can help us bring our ideas to fruition.

Many of us experience moods in which we feel suddenly inspired toward some definite goal, be it writing a novel, taking a university course, or bringing a child into the world. We usually feel strongly about it for a while, often long enough to initiate the scheme, but how often does the inspiration die in infancy? All too often we are left with a few chapters under the bed or on an old hard drive, a lot of boring work we don't want to be bothered with, or a lifestyle whose compromise we resent. It isn't that we've made the wrong choice or committed ourselves in the heat of the moment, it's that we've lost track of the original inspirational plan. We've failed to nurture the seed we have sown.

It is ourselves—especially the Higher Self—we let down when we fail to maintain our dreams. This is a very understandable and common stumbling block; mundanity is often a stronger force than insight or foresight. However, it would be much easier and more positive to be consistent in application of self; Hathor, the most stable and giving figure in the Egyptian pantheon, can help.

Approaching Hathor: Preparation

Unlike the case with many other godforms, to become properly attuned to Hathor it is important to be well earthed. She is indeed a very down-to-earth goddess. An outside walk, some gardening or cooking or any other gentle, practical pursuit can help align you to the wavelength of this Goddess of Beneficence.

Presumably, you have already decided what it is you want to nurture. Ensure it is something of a viable nature—if it is a difficult quest, but something you really wish to attain, fine; if it is totally illogical and lacking in practical foundation, however, Hathor energy will laugh you off. If you have decided your scheme is definitely within the realms of possibility, it is time to present your case to this kind and obdurate deity.

There is no need for breathing exercises or auric aerobics prior to this visualization; they will only put you in an overly mystical frame of mind. Instead, think of the most matriarchal woman you know; not the battle ax variety, but the strong, stable sort who makes sure she protects her own (usually, her family). These women are sometimes lacking in imagination and do not suffer "fools" gladly: i.e., ironically, those of us with unusual inclinations such as high-flying spiritual ideals. Do not be duped into thinking Hathor women are slow, far from it. They demonstrate a shrewd intelligence, particularly when it comes to social politics and money. They can steer the course of their often more creative and dreamy partners, and they are very successful as captains of large family ships. They provide the foundations on which their more expressive offspring flourish. As such, encountering Hathor herself will not lessen your creativity but rather, will help you provide a more stable base from which your creativity can reach new heights. It follows that the more earthed you wish to be, the more you should meditate on this most solid of goddesses.

Visualization for Nurturing a Project

Approach this visualization in a frank and determined frame of mind. You know what you want to do; ensure that you have the power to endure in your endeavor.

Hathor is standing in a kitchen, tending to numerous pots on the stove. Children's voices can be heard in the next room and outside, chattering and laughing. The smell of baking bread permeates the room. Outside, the window branches hang heavy with apples ripening in the sun; flowers overflow their beds. There is a beautifully maintained vegetable garden in the foreground. The house is filled with an atmosphere of well-being.

Hathor glows with a deep yellow aura and halo. The effulgent goddess has the body of a stout human woman, representing her higher intelligence and sublime productivity, but her head and shoulders are those of a cow. A glow is visible on her cheeks. She seems very human but is blessed with a rare tranquility. Her eyes are superficially bovine—certainly imperturbable—but in their reddish-brown depths is a spark of sharp intelligence, of the power to defend. It is intelligence and force in reserve, however.

From her flow astral sustenance as well as physical well-being; she delivers a promise of a bright, safe future. Try to stabilize your own astral body and imagine yourself with your feet planted firmly in Hathor's green garden; your roots extend down from the soles deep into the earth. Feel the power of the earth flowing up into your body, coursing through your veins.

Envision your plan as a small plant or shrub.

Hathor sees you in the garden and comes out to greet you; she wipes her hands on her apron as she emerges.

Stand planted firmly opposite this chimerical goddess. Feel the change in your vibrational rate as it slows to a steady, rudimentary beat. Speak to her mentally in any way you feel inclined. See how she responds. In the event that the response is unfavorable, go away and reconsider your project. Perhaps you can reformat your request into something more acceptable to this most utilitarian of deities.

Still envisioning your project as a sapling, admire Hathor's garden with its fertile soil and flourishing greenery. Communicate your appreciation to her as you do so. Again, listen for any comments and feedback you may get. They may prove useful regarding the concept at hand.

Look again at your young plant and consider how well it would do if installed in Hathor's own verdant garden! Taking as long as you need to explain your cause, ask Hathor if you may plant it here. If she assents, you are halfway to success already.

Envelop your plant in the yellowy aura you have developed in emulation of Hathor's. Send energy to its base and plant it in the soil. Watch as it takes root; the deeper they go, the more definite a place it has in futurity.

Extend your aura and water your plant in whatever way suits you; a jug, or a sudden shower—whatever you prefer—and send it your devotion. Promise to tend to it every day, and to make practical moves in the outside world to bring it to the height of its manifestation. Ask Hathor to tend to it while you are away in the material world. While she babysits your dreamchild, you can create the physical channels to bring it into being.

To really ensure success, visit your "plant" every morning; nurture it and watch it grow. Sometimes it might seem germinal, in which case you need to pump more energy into it. At other times, it will reflect your effort and soon-to-be circumstances by appearing leafy and lustrous. Make sure that every time you visit it, you leave it larger than it was when you arrived; thank Hathor for tending it in your absence. Your dreams will surely come to fruition.

CHAPTER 9

MA'AT

Sobriety is my purpose and my will.

No braggart drunk on delusion can alter my word, though with petty force and unjust laws they try; for in the very definition of my word is the physical realm made manifest.

Those prayers touch me that are pure of motive; to the roar of the ego I am deaf. I am not like children borne of flesh, easily influenced. I am cosmic justice, and all shall know my eternal truth regardless of their hierarchical position.

Said the lost ones: "Mother, we are caught in a nightmare—all we see seems real; Mother, shatter this illusion we do not understand! The knives are real and they make us bleed real blood!"

Let nothing taint your vision of a balanced world; in me, the whole world is made even.

"Some people are crazed, Mother. They inflict injustice as if it were a righteous thing to do. They spread lies and cast in depravity they lean against the scales of Justice and tip them down."

Where is your faith, child?

"Too long have the bright ones burned in the darkness; our resources are all used up! Sometimes our souls are like ashes, self-cremated in the cause of perpetuating inner vision. Mother Ma'at, why do you allow the thieves of righteousness to inhabit the halls of existence?"

Self-pity does not become the servants of the light. Your rectitude is its own reward, though there may be others in the end. See how, even on your level, there are bright pockets of justice sewn into the rough fabric of your lives? Imagine, then, the radiance of those found in the brighter material of the astral and spiritual planes! Never forget, we see all, though every soul you know may be blind. None walks immune, and every heart will be judged according to the eternal laws of truth.

We do not test beyond your means of endurance, so in hardship be honored; it indicates true fortitude of soul.

All will be balanced. All will be made even. This is my promise and my purpose and my will.

Present to me the cause of your crying out and I will stem it at the source if its waters are contaminated.

Remember, the darkness is as sacred as the light, and both are necessary composites for the formulation of a day.

Trust me, for I am as inevitable as the dawn; as logical as alge-
bra. I am the judge and the equalizer and the cosmic conclusion of
all action.
I will not let you down.

MA'AT, OR MAYET, IS the Goddess of Justice, against whose cosmic featherweight all hearts are measured on death. If one has led a good life, the scales will balance, but if they tip, one's heart (i.e., essence) is eaten by the monster Ammut, a chimera from the realms of chaos. Whether the scales tip up or down is not entirely clear; one would expect the bad heart to outweigh the feather through the weight of sin, but some sources indicate that the feather of Ma'at grows heavier if the organ is characterized by deceit. In this instance, the feather outweighs the heart. Personally, I have always construed the feather of Ma'at as being as light as a clear conscience would feel in the circumstance of judgment and therefore outweighed by the guilt-laden heart. For the purposes of this book, I have maintained the latter standpoint. In either instance, imbalance with the feather points to incongruity with the principles of Ma'at. In the same way that a gluttonous or poor diet will eventually destroy the physical body, spiritual annihilation is the consequence natural to the Egyptian mind for acting in opposition to cosmic order. It is not so much a punishment as a mathematical certainty.

Ma'at measures the spiritual vitamin-level of each life, thus determining its longevity. There are numerous criteria involved in this process, from internal and external behavior to the repercussions of actions committed on the earth plane. The balance of the psyche is also paramount; the anima and animus, as we call them today, must be in cooperative working condition. In this era in which we progress from the more traditional Age of Osiris, Ma'at is especially involved in guarding the newly developing balance between male and female forces on the external and internal planes.

Balance, indeed, is the key to the mystery of Ma'at. In geographical terms, she represents the unity of Upper and Lower Egypt, the fertile land and the desert. She also indicates the equipoise between mundane individuality and ego with the Higher Self and its ensuing cosmic overview. She is sometimes referred to as Double Ma'at in respect of this unifying aspect.

Ma'at

Ma'at is the principle of divinity and righteousness, without whom all deteriorates into chaos. The gods themselves are said to "live by Ma'at." Indeed, the breath of light that confers their divinity is the essence of which Ma'at herself is exclusively made. By her very nature, she is just and true; any psychological taints such as egoism, greed, or jealousy are anathema to her. In the negative affirmation of the soul after death, Egyptians were asked to quantify the state of the heart by answering specific questions pertaining to their conduct on earth, about whether they had lied, stolen, or nurtured envy among other things. However, it was the final question that could tip the scales of this matter of conscience and extricate them from the waiting jaws of Ammut. The individual was asked whether there was anyone on earth who was glad they had been born. Even if they are guilty on every other count, they could be redeemed if able to answer this question with conviction. Indeed, clarity of conscience rather than lack of wrong action seemed to be the key to immortality; if one's motivations were right, the heart balanced against the feather. Thus, Ma'at is as kind as she is just; theoretically, the role model of the pharaoh himself. Indeed, in the pharaoh's hand is an effigy of the seated Ma'at, an echo of his own position on the throne.

The consorts of Ma'at in the underworld are Anubis and Osiris, and she is mythologically married to Thoth (Tahuti), who shares her qualities of truth and integrity. Ancient Egyptians were urged to "speak Ma'at and do Ma'at." Morality and the goddess's name were eponymous.

Connected with her spiritual purity is the association of Ma'at with abstinence. Illicit sex or sexual excess and overindulgence in food and intoxicants are particularly repugnant to her. As in many scriptures (notably Hindu and latter-day Christian) only whatever was deemed to purify and strengthen the system could rightfully belong in the ordered world of spiritual integrity. Conversely, Ma'at is linked with fasting; indeed, the quality of lightness itself is integral to Ma'at. Spiritual and physical gluttony will make her scales tip downward and threaten the longevity of the heart and soul.

Many of the principles of Ma'at, and of the philosophical heights of Egyptian justice, are illustrated in the novels of Joan Grant, particularly *Eyes of Horus* (reprinted by Ariel Press). Grant's tales provide an absorbing insight into ancient Egypt with a first-hand narrative; the author herself purports to speak from "far memory."

As judge of karmic repercussions, Ma'at determines whose souls return to earth, whose linger in the demiworlds, and whose are consigned to primordial chaos and destroyed. When relieved of her duties in the underworld, she is said to ride the solar barque during its diurnal journey across the sky. Of course, the divine essence of Ma'at is not confined to any one place at a time. She is equated with all levels of reality and pervades all things at all times. Truth, as we know, is integral to numerous paradigms. However, it is not so much the goddess that concerns us in the following exercise as her weighing equipment—the ubiquitous Libran scales of justice.

A major issue with decision-making is obtaining an objective overview. Ephemeral thoughts and emotions often destroy our capacity to see a situation with clarity—particularly in affairs of the heart, a specialty of Ma'at. The sort of situations in which these visualizations can be particularly helpful are those represented by the Lovers card in the tarot; choices and potential paths that will take us away from whatever we have become accustomed to, or any decision that will have long-term repercussions.

Ma'at is the Goddess of Truth. Some philosophies hold that by speaking the truth, one gains the ability to manifest all words spoken from the heart— the power of *vak* in Hinduism. Ma'at likewise represents the godlike capacity to create on the material planes through will combined with speech, chants, seed-glyphs. As such, she represents a formidable magickal ability. Certainly, the most powerful magick always has its foundations in truth, which makes it unshakable in the winds of change. Truth exists; lies and deception are built on the ever-shifting, shallow sands of emotion. There can be no greater spiritual armor than a clear conscience. Even false accusation—and corrupt persons frequently falsely accuse—will eventually fly in the face of the perpetrator and touch not one iota of a soul of true integrity, except perhaps to make them stronger in the long run.

All power to Ma'at forever and always; AUM!

Ma'at

Encountering Ma'at: Preparation

As Ma'at is a goddess of moderate abstinence, it can be beneficial to undergo a small fast for a day or two before approaching her, perhaps cutting out all but necessary intake. Alternatively, if relevant, you could stop smoking or refuse alcohol. If you normally eat meat, it is always best to forego it for as long as you feel able, though permanently is preferable. One of the principles of Ma'at, universal justice, is vegetarianism/veganism, at least when animal products are not required for survival.

A salt bath is a good idea before this visualization—concentrate on washing yourself clean of superficial preferences and immediate concerns. An incense such as sandalwood or a Libra mix (or if you can find or make it, a Ma'at-specific brand) will be a beneficial accompaniment.

At noon, when the forces of light and darkness are in equilibrium, is a good time to connect with Ma'at; a waxing moon half full or more will also aid the visualization. Dawn and dusk are almost always excellent times for magick.

Visualization for Making Balanced Decisions

Decide on a simple but appropriate symbol for each of the situations between which you are choosing; you could, for example, use a square to represent the life to which you are accustomed, and a star for more aspirational pursuits. We are going to keep this visualization basic for clarity's sake. Chances are, you are already confused and too much symbolic paraphernalia will be far from helpful.

Take several deep, purifying breaths. Imagine the luminous air infiltrating your bodies, starting at the core of your physical one and emanating outward to the peripheries of your etheric and astral body (for the purposes of this exercise, about seven feet from your skin in every direction). As you breathe out, concentrate on expelling from your body all subjectivity and superficial angst or emotion. Inhale light, exhale confusion.

When you feel slightly spacey and your mind is reasonably blank, visualize the balancing scales of Ma'at. They are large and sturdy but inordinately sensitive.

Now, put your symbols in the pans, one on each side, and see what happens. If you have more than two symbols to weigh, use the lightest of the last pair to counterbalance the new symbol.

If the symbols balance, there is nothing to choose between the options—do what you like. If one symbol crashes to the ground or is very heavy, it is a bad idea, inspired by the wrong motives. The lighter the symbol, the better the choice. If you have nothing to weigh your idea against, use the final symbol recommended; that of the white ostrich feather of Ma'at.

To finalize any decision process, weigh the symbol against the Goddess's own symbolic tool of judgment (the feather). Feel the atmosphere of antiquity caught in the feather's shaft and sacred vanes; see how particles of light adhere to it as a whole. This seemingly innocuous item has sent a hundred thousand souls plummeting into Ammut's gullet and dispatched a million more to stellar life and immortality.

If your symbol and the feather of Ma'at balance out equally, all is well and good. If your choice is lighter than the feather, you have made a decision based on higher values; it is a worthy path. If, however, your decision raises the feather above it, you should forget it; it is a morally or psychologically corrupt choice that may bring you eventual regret.

Within a few minutes, you will have made a decision approved by your Higher Self, who has of course longer-term vision than your mundane self. It is now down to your personal discrimination whether you follow it or not.

❀

Ma'at

CHAPTER 10

SEKHMET

Lioness-headed Lady of Fire, hissing her catalysts.

Ferocious with all that might be counter to progress, her scepter, shaped like a cobra, spits light, mesmerizing, confirming her power.

Blithely, her gaze skims her adorants in this palace of sibilant sands, the land of the shaman and shape-shifter. When Sekhmet is displeased, when her children do not honor her by fulfilling their potential, and by the fierce combat of cruelty, all who cannot sustain her interest vanish in a searing flame of feline disdain. She skims their essence from the ether and redecorates the rooms of her mind, her palace of astral wonder. From this spring new connections and processes, perchance civilizations.

The paint of her magickal art is always wet, for Sekhmet changes her creations by the moment. Each spark of light in her leonine head is captured and remolded with magicks of precision and perfection and then made manifest.

Such is the eternal potential of the lioness who is one of the Great Ones.

SEKHMET WAS ORIGINALLY CAST in the Egyptian pantheon as upholder of cosmic order, of the wills of her father Ra of the sun and of divine justice, Ma'at. Distinctively depicted with her regal lioness's head, she is a great military figurehead and patroness. Sekhmet's red-hot weapons of darts and arrows and her ability to scorch were used to cauterize and deflect evil and keep it at bay. She is the Eye of Ra who guards against all wrongdoing, the "Great Lady, beloved of Ptah," her brother and husband. Sometimes she is deemed wife and sister of Seth, with whom she shares many fiery traits. Sekhmet is often depicted carrying a life-affirming ankh, showing that the "strength, might and violence"—the meaning of her name—are used to virtuous ends. Her other symbols include the solar disk headdress, red attire, the sistrum, and the uraeus. Sekhmet is the youngest child of the celestial sky herself, Nuit (Nut), and her own sons are Nefertem (Purity) and Heka (Magick). As fire destroys and regenerates, as heat cleanses and as the alchemist's alembic distills, so too does Sekhmet's sacred flame affect mind, body, and soul.

At some juncture, the fearsome aspect of Sekhmet became the pronounced trait in lieu of her divine rectitude; retribution was replaced by gratuitous gore, and she came to symbolize the destructive forces of Seth and was to be worshipped in conjunction with him. This notwithstanding, the aspect of Sekhmet that is fierce and bloodthirsty is in fact the ferociousness of justice. As a sexual goddess associated with heat, and thus with the powers of *sekhem* or kundalini, the connection may have arisen through Seth's affiliation with the Upper Nile, and powers of fire and the sun at its most destructive, and/or from the practice of orgiastic rites in her honor. Sekhmet was at times deemed to preside over harmful magick; Joan Grant's novel *Eyes of Horus* gives an imaginatively lurid vision of her worship at the height of its reputed depravity. In reality, the destructive side of Sekhmet, as with many deities, is a necessary natural force.

In her entirely positive aspect, this goddess—by far the greatest of the many Egyptian godforms depicted with the head of a lion—represents the qualities of protection, healing, grace, and a keen intelligence. Her sharp senses are especially honed to detect any threat to her own; she is a particularly patriotic and loyal deity. She was often prayed to for destruction of enemies, particularly the Nubian tribes, and her weapons included a fire-tongued cobra and the Seth-like power to parch. She is endowed with searing insight. Majestic in black basalt, Sekhmet is undemonstrative about her unquestionable strength. Her shrine at Karnak draws dedicants and worshippers to this very day, echoing the theme of regenerative force.

Sekhmet is associated with Ptah, Sculptor of the Universe, and with Ra, sometimes appearing in the form of a uraeus (holy cobra) on the brow of the latter. She is the heat of midday that destroys pestilence with her fiery breath. Produced as an embodiment of Hathor's fury, she is her polar antithesis—where Hathor nurtures, Sekhmet destroys. Where Hathor is placid and gives milk, Sekhmet is thirsty for blood. This blood can be menstrual also, a symbol of both fertility and of feminine power, and a secretion of magickal import (possibly connected symbolically with the *tyet* of Isis). Sekhmet's guile, feline energy and grace epitomize the cunning accredited by the Egyptians to the harbingers of chaos, the flipside of the dignified holy chimera. And yet, she was also rightfully recognized as much more than destruction: indeed, her ambivalent nature represents flexibility and adaptability not dissimilar to that of Kali, and on a lower key, to many of the highly dualistic Greek deities.

In *Sekhmet: Transformation in the Belly of the Goddess* (2017), Nicki Scully suggests presenting one's personal fear, grief, and pain to Sekhmet as offerings for a feast of inner transformation. As psychologist Jeffrey Mishlove writes of her take on Sekhmet as goddess: "This goddess refuses to be forgotten. She serves as a hierophant or bridge to a world of vast psychic potentialities." This

Sekhmet

ancient healer and sorceress, who even held precedence over Osiris and the underworld during times of flooding and storms, is as powerful today as ever she was—versatility is one of her most notable features.

Because of her fluidity and perfect attunement to the animal kingdoms, coupled with her higher intelligence, Sekhmet is a superb shamanic totem. She can be approached as an aide to powers of insight, empathy, and camouflage. These qualities are of great use when astrally traveling, for example; particularly when one is on a particular mission. During psychic attack, the art of disguise is invaluable, as it enables one to travel to the source of the mischief, identify it, and hopefully deflect and stem it off.

Sekhmet's incredible alertness is another quality relevant to magickal endeavor. She never daydreams or misses a trick; watching a lioness with her cubs will demonstrate this; she combines the ideal traits of unflinching observation, grace, and power.

Lions being the majestic symbol of the sun, as well as the kings and queens of the jungle, Sekhmet could be termed a solar warrior. "Lion-heartedness" is habitually associated with generosity and an all-embracing nature (often with a soft center; see *The Wizard of Oz* or Aslan of *The Chronicles of Narnia*); but Sekhmet, being both female and of the cat family, is discriminating in her favor. She does not lack generosity but neither is she a pushover. Needless to say, she evinces the usual feline traits of arrogant courage coupled with cunning, sensuality, and fierce protectiveness.

Traditionally, the solar domain is male-dominated and materialistic. It is the city of culture and commerce, the active yang, as opposed to the arcady of lunar femininity, the receptive yin. However, as Sekhmet is solar *and* feminine, she combines the qualities of both camps, as an enhanced macrocosm of the human psyche; or, arguably, the human psyche being a diminished projection of original consciousness. Lady Sekhmet is a multifaceted deity who lends herself to a variety of situations practical and magickal. For the purposes of this book, however, it is her shamanic aspect on which we focus.

Shamanic Ability: Preparation

Shape-shifting is no mere fantasy; an adept can mimic the shape and form of any animal they choose (but the greater the fondness and knowledge of that form, the better)—anything from a hornet to a horse. They are, however, usually detectable. The hornet, for example, is likely to be bigger and noisier than the ordinary insect, and shape-shifters often have a shimmering edge if you look properly. In the weirdest case scenario, the animal form will bear the face of the person within. They are, after all, an astral chimera.

The following may test the credulity level of some readers, who will perhaps hypothesize hypnotism or illusion as a possible source, but there are many who have witnessed such feats and even participated in them, including myself. Admittedly it can be an alarming experience at first, but fascination usually surpasses fear in such circumstances. This exercise, however, is designed to expand one's astral wardrobe and create an array of animal avatars, rather than to physically manifest animal-forms, though the line between the two is thin.

You do not need to take a special bath or shower prior to this visualization, but a pinch of suitable incense on a charcoal disk could be helpful for clearing and attuning your space.

Visualization for Shamanic Ability

Sit comfortably with your spine as straight as possible, or lie supine if you can guarantee not to fall asleep. Use whichever position best facilitates astral travel and vivid inner vision.

Imagine all of your seven major chakras spinning in unison, counterclockwise and then clockwise, with a propeller-like action. They whirr faster and faster, lifting your astral body away from the physical one and carrying it high into the air like a helicopter, filling the atmosphere with the sound of AUM.

As your astral body rises, try directing it. By concentrating on your crown and pineal chakras you can rise vertically into the air, while increased spinning of your lower chakras will even you out. Experiment for yourself, not forgetting to envision the color of each "propeller."

Now, imagine that the action of the chakras begins to produce a gossamer substance a bit like protoplasm. Feel it cocoon and pulsate around you. This substance comes from you and is infinitely pliant to your own will. It will encase you in any form you choose—hawk, wolf, serpent, or otherwise. Perhaps an astral body will begin to form without your conscious volition. Whichever animal you wish to become, attune your third eye to the third eye area of a mental image of that animal. First be its mirror image, then *become* it.

Try shifting your shape through a variety of forms and move accordingly. If you feel yourself fading or falling, take light from the ether and use it to sustain you.

As you become each animal, really try to think like it. Keep thoughts basic, sensual-raw, and elemental. If you are an eagle, feel the spread of your wings, the breezes and winds that are your ley lines, your mastery of air, and your total belonging to this element. You might feel a keen hunger and find your vision piercing the hedgerows and fields far below for the movement of some tender morsel. You may just soar and swoop for the pleasure of it; feel the zephyrs in your feathers.

As a wolf, smell the pine trees, the freshness of snow, and sense the hum of distant blood. Feel the pheromone network of your pack around you; your instinctive understanding of rhythm and vibration in the earth; and of snort, glance, growl, and howl. Feel the heavy fur on your back; a pelt of camouflage as well as warmth. Feel the pad of your paws on the redolent earth. Run and test your muscle power; feel the strength and health of your four limbs as they pound the ground, snapping twigs and scattering damp leaves and needles. Silently acknowledge the spirits of shelter and quarry; the only gods you know beneath the cold starry sky.

If you are a serpent, wriggle on your limbless belly; feel how all your power is concentrated into one thin line of tactile spine. No longer dissipated, your patterned flesh is potent and honed to the single cause of your razor-sharp will. Exercise your authority with a warning, or hiss and rise up to strike the enemy. Feel every inch of your sibilant elasticity; the snaking S of your backbone; the thick flakes of flesh packed around it. Attune yourself to reptile mythology; how misunderstood and maligned your kind have been! Your python-self hooded the Buddha, after all, and your forefathers helped churn the lost amrita from the celestial Indian seas. What thanks do you get? None at all. It makes you spit.

For Sekhmet, the obvious choice is the lioness. To experiment successfully with this form, you should concentrate on graceful alacrity, alertness, and majesty. Your unflinching poise reflects your pride and confidence.

❦

Nothing can perturb you, for all else is far, far beneath you. You are sleek with agile feline arrogance. Your teeth and powerful limbs ensure your rule is perpetuated. The atavistic traits of the infinitely superior cat family are made manifest in you, beautiful and mighty one.

You luxuriate with self-satisfaction until a movement in the grass provokes a sudden, violent fury. You kill the small animal without a second thought, punishing it for daring to exist in your domain. The little dose of sweet blood tastes good. You will hunt more if you get bored.

Do not forget to keep those chakras whirring and glowing, no matter how the colors have faded and changed. It is good to envision them working inside your animal body covered by the relevant skin or pelt and thus invisible.

When you have finished experimenting, slow your chakras down and re-absorb the substance from which you created your animal forms. If you like, you can keep them as they are and envision your aura as containing a compartment like a walk-in wardrobe. You may need to upgrade or rework parts of the animal form the next time you put it on, but most of its form will remain, with any luck.

With constant practice, shapeshifting will become second nature, and you will be able, like all good shamans, to walk at will between worlds. The more frequently you masquerade in your animal costume, the better it will fit. You will find new perceptions flooding your senses as you begin to exchange energies with the animal genus concerned. This firsthand encounter with the animal kingdom certainly beats the more conventional methods of experiencing the diminishing world of nature.

Sekhmet

PART III

GREEK GODDESSES

CHAPTER 11

ARTEMIS

No man has ever touched this sacred flesh, molded by my will. Let no man ever touch it.

No will has ever dominated my will. Let no will ever taint it.

No hunter's bow has dispatched arrows with the surety of mine. Let none exceed me.

No cunning beast has ever outwitted my wit. Let none elude me.

No legs have ever outpaced my swift strong legs. Let none outpace me.

No being has ever crossed me and survived. Let no one cross me.

No eye has ever scanned my virginity and blinked again. Let all be blind who observe me.

I am Zeus's daughter, protector of women and young girls, divine huntress and Olympian athlete supreme.

I am eternally young and rightfully proud. None may displease me and expect to live.

Be warned, all ye who would sin against women and hold my daughters in contempt: ye shall be hunted down like quarry and thrown to the dogs.

Be warned, all women who ally yourselves with wrongful forces: even those of you who call yourselves my daughters. Treat your own kind with respect or you shall be doubly punished.

For I am Artemis Hecaerge, who shoots from afar and never misses. From me, though you may dodge behind trees and linger in tangled thicket, there is no hope of escape; for the pursuit of the uncivilized is my sport and only pleasure.

DAUGHTER OF ZEUS AND Leto, Artemis is the boyish girl of the Greek myths; often she displays more classically masculine traits than her twin brother Apollo. Though often regarded as a lunar deity, Artemis is indeed rooted in logic and action. Her militant independence and uncompromising absorption in sporting activities create a female prototype unparalleled in other pantheons, and one with strong solar as well as lunar affiliations.

However, this spiritually potent dualism is irrelevant to the nonbinary Artemis unless it catalyzes and enhances action. She is a goddess devoid of the introspective urge, choosing rather to mirror the natural, animal world in which she runs free; a domain in which empathy between hunter and hunted would cause dysfunction. Blithely she is described in the Homeric hymn to Artemis as "sending forth shafts of sorrow" as she "turns about on every side slaying the race of wild beasts." In an epoch during which wild animals were rife and humanity was always under threat from the natural world, Artemis as hunter represented a civilizing, balancing force. Her apparent selfishness in hunting—certainly out of kilter with today's circumstances of animal plight and extinction—was to the ancient Greek as essential to her as her bow, arrows, and hunting tunic. We are told that she slays also those who kill sacred animals; her role is, in addition, protective. She is a balanced part of nature.

Artemis defies both Hellenistic and modern gender stereotypes, flaunting the expectations of society as a whole. Relentless in the pursuit of pleasure and excellence, the force of her will carries her above the groupmind that would categorize, integrate, and neutralize her. She operates alone, strong in her androgyny and eternal youth. Her mental and spiritual growth were arrested at adolescence; one might even say at spiritual prepubescence. She is the tomboy teenager who never grows up. Refusing to end the charmed and exhilarating adventures of childhood, Artemis is fiercely chaste, mercilessly slaying sexual transgressors and even those like Actaeon who accidentally glimpse her with her modesty compromised. For this incident, Ovid describes how the tragic Greek hero is turned into a stag and subsequently torn to shreds by his own hunting dogs. As a warrior, Artemis helps destroy the serpent Python and avenges the rapes of her protégée nymphs. She sanitizes any ensuing births, removing the "miasma" of Grecian taboo.

At play, Artemis loves nothing more than running free in the woods with her swift, strong pack, on the scent of some wild quarry. With her lean body, narrow-hipped and minimally chested, the ability to flout the feelings and opinions of the other gods with neither qualm nor guilt, and her pristine concentrated will, Artemis is the supreme athletic archetype. This lithe exemplar of holistic agility is an ideal role model for those with sporting aspirations, particularly serious ones. Athletics demand many of the traits Artemis so effortlessly exhibits—the ability to train relentlessly and the consequent foregoing of emotional preoccupations. There could be no better goddess to whom to appeal in matters physically competitive or demanding, or for any feat requiring precision and stamina. The same is true for the certainty and confidence to be defined by character and not gender or sexuality. Self-belief and self-discipline are gifts she bestows, including that which helps befit the body to receive divine boons; thus she opens one up to divine interaction.

In the Homeric Hymns, Artemis is described as a keen and gracious dancer: having tired of the hunt, "then she arrays the lovely dance of Muses and Graces...graciously clad about she leads the dances, first in place...," Thus she is depicted in the aspect of a courtly goddess, skilled in the civilised arts, not simply as a tomboy running wild in the woods.

The traits described here are in stark contrast to those of Artemis of Ephesus, the Great Mother and symbol of fertility that pertains more to the Phrygian Kybele and Babylonian Ishtar, among other such forms. The visually baffling multibreasted Ephesian Artemis demonstrates a fascinating conjunction of cultural, religious, and practical concepts that do not directly concern us here. The interested reader is referred to *Artemis of the Ephesians: Mystery, Magic, and Her Sacred Landscape* by James D. Rietveld, whose emphasis is on the mystery and spiritually relevant aspects of this figure and her place in everyday Ephesian life, as well as this particular aspect's universality.

The classical Grecian Artemis on whom we are focused in this chapter is a particularly appropriate totemic deity independent for women, especially those who prefer one another's company to that of men, family, or children. She is a protector of other boyish girls and has a strong distaste for the kind of flighty behavior engendered by Aphrodite. This goddess is not averse to marriage per se, but when this occurs, the participating woman must abandon her childhood memorabilia at Artemis's altar, consecrate her tunics to the maiden goddess, and leave the merry troupe of huntresses for good.

At childbirth, however, Artemis may appear again, her knowledge of instinctive matters aiding her ex-protégée through her tribulations. Bearing a flaming pine-torch symbolic of protective warmth, Artemis Phaesporia brings light and welcomes the newborn infant into the world. Many women in ancient Greece prayed to Artemis as the celestial midwife for pain relief and a swift, safe delivery. Mythologically, she is often said to have helped deliver her own twin brother, Apollo, when their mother Leto was being harassed by the ever-jealous Hera, who, according to Hygenus, would not allow her to give birth on any earth or anywhere under the sun. Eventually the demure Leto managed to bear forth her children on the floating island of Delos. Perhaps this enmity from Zeus's queen underlies Artemis's dislike of—nay, disdain for—heterosexual interaction; her own mother's affair with a married god caused continual upheaval for all concerned, as did her father's numerous romantic dalliances.

Certainly, the Hellenistic Artemis holds no shrift with such silliness; her preoccupations are with dignity, strength, and sporting ability. As huntress and inhabitant of the forest she is known by Homer as Artemis Agrotera, Artemis the Huntress of Wild Animals. This lithe deity is also beautiful and proud of her looks; physical perfection is another of Artemis's domains. However, this self-nurturing goddess expresses nothing that is not primarily for her own pleasure. Narcissism and unwillingness to please others is the root of any vanity she and her priestesses harbor. Artemis will aid change if this comes of one's own volition rather than to please others or simply to fit in.

The criticisms of others, even those subconsciously stashed at the motivational root, will be disparaged and disregarded by Artemis, whose hauteur exists even vicariously, so carefully analyze your reasons for conducting the visualizations for changing body shape. Neuroses do not impress this caustic, down-to-earth goddess, so best avoid petitioning her on their behalf.

Approaching Artemis: Preparation

As Artemis is a maiden goddess, the new moon is a propitious time to access her. Like Hecate, she is a light-bearer, and the flaming torch is included in both goddesses' symbolism: lanterns and candles are therefore particularly relevant to her.

Cedar and pine oil, or a combination of moon and sun incense, will also be of benefit.

A cool, bracing shower will help—it is important to feel pristine and capable prior to these meditations.

Visualization for Changing Body Shape

For fitness purposes, concentrating on the throat chakra helps metabolize etheric energy through the medulla oblongata, lessening the desire and need for food. Few techniques can beat a healthy diet in conjunction with meditational yoga and regular exercise.

The etheric body, surrounding and merging with the physical body, contains the specifications for physical growth, as directed by the Higher Self and tailored by current thought processes and attitudes. The Higher Self may not have intended for us to have a stooped back, for example, but years of low self-esteem, working slumped over a desk, or even feeling too awkwardly tall may have caused it to become so. Many illnesses, being almost without exception emotionally and spiritually psychosomatic (even the most serious) begin in the etheric aura—thus, by keeping the aura clean, it is possible to dramatically reduce the chance of illness. Likewise, by manipulating the aura and maintaining a relevant mental attitude, the shape of the physical body may be altered, as it always follows where the etheric body leads. This is the principle behind the motto "think tall"; lofty attitudes and spiritual attainments can literally increase one's height.

First, formulate your plan: a healthy plant-based diet and regular exercise are the two most obvious ingredients for success.

Now stand before a full-length mirror by dim light. A low-watt bulb or candlelight are good, but the natural light of dawn or dusk is particularly perfect for magickal transformation processes.

You should be able to clearly see the parts of your body you are adjusting, so either work naked or scantily clad; whichever feels best to you.

Burn a little sun and moon incense together or evaporate some cedar or pine oil to help evoke the swift and slender goddess Artemis.

Try to avoid mentally adopting the drifty, nebulous atmosphere that pervades in these "between" times. You will be employing its qualities to define your new body shape but should remain mentally taut, like Artemis, and grounded in the physical.

Turn sideways so that the mirror reflects your right shoulder, and take several slow, deep breaths. With each inhalation, charge yourself up with blue-white energy.

Contemplate the angular, boyish goddess with her fresh complexion, hunting tunic above the knees, bow in hand. The straps of her quiver are slung across her chest, and inside this container you perceive a golden glow. Although Artemis's aura is often red (she received many blood sacrifices in arcane times in respect of her hunting aspect), when approached in her youngest form and as you concentrate on her youthful exhilaration while running through the pine forests, her exuberant liberty, she emits a silvery green glow. This is the Artemis whose help we wish to engender, so envision her as such.

Visualize a silvery green luminescence before you, slightly fir- and pine-scented. Breathe it in and out until you feel attuned to it. From this phosphorescence, witness the solid beginning to grow. See Artemis's bearskin-shod feet, fleet as the wind, immaculately attuned to her mental command. See her sleek, strong legs, toned and honed to her will, capable of carrying her effortlessly, almost unconsciously, through forest, down vale, and over hill in the thrill of the chase.

Note the narrow hips girded with the chamois-colored hunting pelt; various throat-slitting tools at her waist. The golden arrows in the case emit a sunbeam-like radiance. All of Artemis's features are streamlined for maximum speed: nothing is merely decorative; all is utilitarian.

See the arms, slim and strong, hued and burnished by the sun. The tendons are taut, poised to act in response to visual perception; but ease, the ease of confidence, permeates the celestial tomboy's stance.

Artemis's hair may be long, as envisioned by poets and artists throughout the ages, but she wears it as if short, defying impractical tresses. The sky-blue eyes scan the air and earth in continual alertness; an inner intelligence interweaves the sounds and motions of realms both animal and human. The goddess Artemis moves effortlessly between the two, as fluent in instinct as she is in logic.

You may be aware of the hunting pack flanking the deity, but there is no need to visualize it unless you wish to. Artemis rarely travels far without her loyal and well-groomed dogs.

Having breathed in her silver-green light, you are already connected to Artemis; strengthen the bond by taking one more deep breath of the wilderness goddess's light. Feel your body, mind, and spirit being infiltrated by her untamed qualities of faultless instinct and independence; her childlike absorption in her own pursuits. Allow the silver-green light to permeate into and emanate from you. Envisage yourself and Artemis coexisting inside this auric tent.

Now, turn to face the mirror and half-close your eyes. Envision your body the way you would like it to be. Formulate your peripheral vision into the shape you aspire to attain. As already mentioned, this is done easiest by dusk or candlelight, when you borrow shadows to help define the right proportions. Exaggerate the details in order to firmly impress them on your will and subconscious: you may even mentally caricature your future self.

Holding this etheric blueprint firmly in your mind's eye, ask for Artemis's help in attaining it. Imagine how good you will feel when you have it and allow these positive feelings to flow into you now. As you continue to tailor your vision to your inner dictate, be aware of your body complying to it also.

Starting at the feet and moving up through ankles and calves, slowly flex your muscles and tendons and watch the two images merge. Where relevant, parallel your self-image to that of Artemis. Do not move until you can clearly see each part of your body conforming to your will. You are telling it what to do, giving it the new mold to which the atoms composing your physical body will comply.

Continue this process right up to your head, and with the determination of Artemis, feel the energy of your new body, the confidence it will create, and know that this is your real future. Then embark upon the physical regime you have planned to help achieve it.

Repeat this exercise as often as possible, preferably once at morning, noon, and night. The more you surround yourself with this enthusiastically created body mold, the sooner your body cells will comply to it. You might also try walking around as if your body were already the way you want it to be. You are, after all, merely projecting yourself into your own not-too-distant future.

Visualization for Sporting Ability and Fitness

As before, stand in a full-length mirror, either naked or in your swimming costume or sports clothes—whatever is most comfortable. Either way, make sure you can see all the muscles you wish to develop.

First, visualize clearly what you wish to achieve. If you are a pole-vaulter, see yourself gliding effortlessly over a high bar in a blaze of glory (hear people gasping and clapping if you so desire); if you are a gymnast, visualize yourself involved in feats of amazing stamina and suppleness. Most likely, you are just aiming for general fitness; in which case, envision your body exhibiting relevant qualities. Whatever your particular aim, the five stages of the following visualization will help you attain it.

The Five Ss

The ingredients for success in the fitness and sporting arena are: suppleness, strength, speed, stamina, and surety. The latter refers to accuracy in aiming, be it yourself, your javelin, ball, or bat. Cool confidence obviously helps attain a spot-on shot, hence the term surety.

Again, visualize your body the way you want it to be. Promise yourself that you will become it. It does not hurt to exaggerate your visions to get your point across—for example, if you are looking for better muscle definition, you could imagine yourself absolutely bulging with muscles. Don't worry if that's not exactly what you want; it impresses the subconscious more if the image is striking and over the top.

Concentrate on Artemis until you feel her in the room with you. Feel the vigor emanating from her, her pitiless ambition, her perfect will. Like Artemis, you will let nothing come between you and your determination to succeed.

Watch yourself in the mirror and begin to concentrate on suppleness. Imagine that all of your limbs are snakes, infinitely tactile like the supreme reptile Python himself. Moving smoothly, emulate the serpent's silent slither. Enjoy the suppleness of your limbs for as long as it feels comfortable.

When you are ready, visualize the ultra confident huntress's body of Artemis as your own, and stretch your limbs as if throwing a spear, drawing your bow, or stalking your prey. Like her, believe that you will never miss a shot. It is merely a matter of how perfect your feat of perfection will be.

Now, center on the faculty of strength. In times of crisis, people have been known to perform incredible feats; for example, women have lifted cars off of their hapless offspring. Clearly, extreme physical power is of a psychospiritual origin, but the trick is not to require a disaster to precipitate it; instead, have the confidence and determination available at all times, including when you are involved in your sporting events and activities, of course.

Continue to stand in front of the mirror; now imagine you are a bear. This animal is sacred to Artemis and is a symbol of strength. Using the bear as a totem, you are going to imagine yourself holding the whole room up.

If possible, stand in a door frame to perform this part of the visualization; another option is to use hand weights to really feel the strain of your efforts. With feet planted apart at shoulder width, hold the weights aloft or push against the top of the doorframe as if you were supporting the roof of the room; as you do, concentrate on your incredible fortitude and bear-like brawn. Even if you are small, you can think big; as already mentioned, strength is not necessarily a function of the physical constitution. Imagine Artemis standing, holding the body of a slaughtered monster high in an exhibition of fortitude and prowess. The pain you feel is an acknowledgment that your muscles are conforming to your mental image and will, so welcome it.

For stamina, continue this pose for as long as you feel apt. Make sure that when you stop, you feel able to strike this pose again and again, only you are choosing *not* to do so. It is good to push yourself to the limit but not to the breaking point. Do not wait until you are weak with exertion, but quit while you are ahead, impressing upon your subconscious the fact that your strength knows no limits. Self-belief is half the composition of stamina.

Meanwhile, indefatigable Artemis is, of course, continuing in her tireless rounds of sporting activities. Stamina is not difficult to acquire when enthusiasm is combined with confidence.

For speed, imagine yourself streamlined like an arrow, being shot from Artemis's bow. Visualize yourself as a brilliant golden streak blessed with powers of incredible alacrity, outdistancing your competitors at the starting shot. As you watch yourself in the mirror, concentrate on how your limbs will lend themselves to the faculty of swiftness. You might also see yourself as Artemis involved in the chase; her only focus is the quarry; she is blissfully unaware of her body and simply homing in on the beast or monster concerned.

The final S is for surety. Envision yourself as somebody who never misses the bull's-eye; somebody whose body is naturally drawn toward the goal. The goddess in this aspect was worshipped as *Artemis Hecaerge*, "the far shooter." From any distance, she can strike the goal. If you play football, *be* the football being kicked into the net. If you are a runner, feel the swift magnetic pull that

Chapter 11

draws your body through the finishing ribbon. You are like a bee making its way from flower to hive; a matter of instinct rather than navigation.

Consider the sharpness of your perceptions: the perfected ability to feel, hear, see, smell, taste, and instinctively attain the coveted goal. Most importantly, continue these exercises on a regular basis, preferably before you train. Refuse inwardly to acknowledge any inadequacies; have total faith in your abilities. Of course, you must work on weak points, but they do not detract from your overriding competence.

Thus we may self-develop, with Artemis as totem and role model. Difficulties are inevitable; only gods are born with their ability in full form. Mystics and yogis practice various sciences of meditation and yoga for decades before they are able to wrestle tigers, lie on beds of nails, or levitate; but eventually they can. Know that with every visualization and every training session and with every ounce of effort, you are drawing nearer to your crowning success.

CHAPTER 12

PERSEPHONE

Pale hands and long fingers; artistic, my mother used to say. Supple as a willow, with that soft pearlescent hue.

Even then, I was silver instead of gold. It seems there is no escaping the Fates.

I liked to spin a tale or two myself: singing, mirrored, and by moonlight I wove my dreams and symbols into mats and cloths and placed them in my mother's halls. Flora and Proserpina or Queen of the Dead; my various personae.

I already knew, you see.

"The girl's insane," some said, but I'd had a presentiment of Pluto. I used my long, lined palms to shake the bones, and from these bones I divined my capture. A noose of black hair fell across my right eye and snaked about my throat.

"Nothing can be done," my friend the Oracle smiled. "Your future belongs to your past, Persephone." She had an annoying habit of speaking in oxymorons; she thought it made her sound more convincing. Her tutor the Sphinx taught it to her.

Hecate stood by with her pack of dog stars, nodding as if everything we said she knew already; it was only natural. She looked very mysterious, though, when I probed her further. "It will be," she said. I could've screamed.

It was Hecate the torch bearer who told my mother of my whereabouts after the abduction. She spied him out, wily crone that she is; she heard my cries. My own father gave me as a gift to be raped.

I wish that she, or anybody living, were here now.

My loneliness echoes through the chambers of Hades; my husband hears it and is affronted. Even as a child bride crowned Queen of the Underworld, he felt my duress as a strain on his heart, and turned an accusatory eye on me. He wields a stinging whip of guilt; down here, it is easy to forget where real truth lies.

I should, he says, be soft and pliant like the flower-gatherer he originally knew. I dare not tell him that no stalagmite, no ancient moss, no dripping lichen can console me for the loss of my mother's feats of fragrant grace: narcissi, hibiscus blossoms—words like spells of bright spring flowers cast upon the rich green earth. He cannot make me happy with his solemn declarations of love eternal, nor with his gloom-embued love-tokens and gifts of baleful power… but I have learned to watch.

I watch the souls of the newly dead arrive by boat; anxious captives awaiting their fate. I give them orders and as I do, I try to gain

❀

Chapter 12

some sense of what is going on above. Sometimes, if they died out-side, I can smell the sunlight in their spirit-hair. With these, for old time's sake, I share a drink.

The dead brew a bitter draft in the recesses of my husband's do-main. It tastes of wormwood and regret; temporarily, it helps us for-get our present and like giddy revenants on the midnight staircase, revisit our past. I used to use it all the time, until I found that it was nibbling nasty little holes into my soul. Now I touch seldom a drop. I have become quite ascetic in my tastes. Possibly—probably—1have been down here for too long.

I await my release with patience, however. I have established a dim subterranean order in my life, and now the upper world seems a chaos of color and noise. Even my mother's corn-colored hair, once my delight to stroke and braid, seems a brazen blaze to my dilated vision. I have learned a thousand shades of gray, the differing tex-tures of shadows.

My spiritforms will miss me when I go, but I know my due. I will sup at a more wholesome cup; I will get my share of sunlight in my hair.

But always, always, no matter where I am, I must return. My present is always my past, and my past my future.

Such is the rotation of the Wheel of Life.

As a child, Persephone lived in her mother Demeter's domain among the fruitful fields and groves of Mount Olympus. She was known as *Kore*, sim-ply meaning maiden, and was surpassingly beautiful. Demeter sent her to earth to protect her from the lustful advances of the other gods; some accounts claim that she went to Sicily. Her key role in Hellenistic mythology and religion is described primarily in the Homeric hymn to Demeter.

Pluto, dark god of the underworld (Hades/Erebus), her father Zeus's brother, was among the admirers of Kore. He asked for her hand in marriage, but sunny Demeter was aghast at the idea of her child steeped in the shadows of the dead and refused. But Pluto was in love with the girl, so together with

Persephone

Zeus, hatched a plan to separate her from Demeter and the nymphs who guarded Kore when her mother was absent.

One day when she was out gathering flowers, Pluto placed a beautiful, beguiling bloom in a field away from her companions, and she fell for the trick. Alone and helpless, she could do nothing but scream as Pluto emerged from a cleft in the earth and snatched her away to the underworld. He subsequently forced her to become his Queen.

In a later version of the myth, she is spotted by the nymph Cyane, who cries so hard at the sight that she becomes a river.

Demeter, deeply distressed by the abduction of her daughter, wandered the earth in desolation, until she came to rest in Queen Metaneira's palace in Eleusis. In disguise and still befuddled by grief, she became the ailing baby prince's nursemaid until, surprised in an attempt to confer immortality on him by placing him in the fire, she angrily revealed her true identity to the horrified Metaneira: for more on this, see the Demeter chapter.

From then on, Demeter's mourning reached new depths, and she withdrew the faculty of fecundity that had kept the soils rich and the leaves green on the trees, causing an instant, interminable winter. With the nature goddess refusing her bounty, it looked as if all might starve unless the earth mother was consoled by her daughter's safe return.

Eventually, with Hermes and Iris as intercessors, a compromise was reached. In some versions this is made easier by Persephone's newfound love for her captor, infuriating Demeter but easing Persephone's own plight. Either way, she has eaten seeds of a pomegranate while in Hades and, consequently, cannot leave it permanently even if she wished to. Thus an agreement is made that she be returned to earth for six months of each year, but abide in Hades for the other six, at least according to Ovid. Other versions of the myth proffer different proportions, while the earlier Homeric hymn suggests three months of annual underworld duty. The principle remains the same. A "time share" would restore Demeter to her rightful state of beneficence long enough for humans to stock up to tide themselves over the barren months.

So, during spring and summer, Persephone walks with her mother and enjoys release from the weighty solemnity of the underworld. During late

❀

autumn and winter, however, she is duty-bound and possibly love-bound to preside over the realms of the dead, whose secrets she knows and whose welfare is her responsibility.

Persephone's childhood has a Satya Yuga–like quality from which her pending womanhood elicits an initiatory fall from joyful innocence similar to the later Christian creation myth. Her early life is idyllic, spent in guileless enjoyment and living in the light; but when her sexuality becomes pronounced, and she becomes desired as a material object, she is instantly transferred to the dark realms of fear and confusion. Kore the maiden is snatched from grace by a desire over which she has no control; consequently, one of the psychological features she represents is that of strong subconscious urges, especially those with drastic repercussions. On one level, Persephone has become trapped in the realization of her body and its powers and functions: she has fallen from the high vibration of innocence into the low, slow vibration of material enslavement. The underworld represents the entrapment of the physical plane; the godless realms of drudgery and negative thought that often mark our transition into adulthood, or reality. Demeter's domain is symbolic of the original god-informed state, the Satya Yuga, Lumurian/Atlantean eras, or biblical Eden, in which thoughts were elevated and physicality barely relevant. This is the tale of innocence and experience of the Greek myths, and there is no doubt that Persephone gains in wisdom what she loses in liberty, however unjust the cause.

Persephone's descent into the underworld is the psychic and psychological initiation referred to in the Eleusinian Mysteries. She raises herself from victim to psychopomp, from hapless child to wise and tacit priestess, becoming her own source of light in the profound darkness of the underworld. Ultimately, she becomes conversant in both realms, with power within each. This is a suitable allegory for the level we inhabit, composed of contrasts and duality—a realm in which, unless we know darkness, we cannot truly appreciate light, where pleasure is redoubled by the previous experience of and release from pain.

Persephone's demi-release from Hades also represents her ability, gleaned in the occult gloom of the underworld, to release herself at least partially from the bondage of materialism and the flesh. The magic she learns in Hades is of

Persephone

transcendence—she realizes that spiritual strength comes from a source independent of external stimuli and physical manifestations.

The myth of Persephone also symbolizes the process of self-realization; a nosedive into the murkiest aspects of the dense material plane and its concomitant ego and psyche. Here, the inner treasures of strength and transcendence brought to the surface. The Hades experience is much akin to crossing the abyss in magickal terms: facing and conquering one's fears and phantoms. Though we have fallen from grace—whether this be symbolized by the Biblical Eden, the Hindu Satya Yuga, or the Atlantean Era—we are not entirely bound. By processes of solitude, magick, and meditation (mantric is purported to be the most effective form of yoga in this era), we can ascend once more into the light and liberation of the original soul-state, like Persephone. Even the most unenlightened being escapes to the soul refuge and recharge point in dreamless sleep and between incarnations. How much more powerful, then, to bring it through consciously!

Consequently, Persephone's gifts are those of sublimating depression into epiphany and rebirth, and the wisdom thus engendered. One undergoes the trials and tribulations of the underworld, receives knowledge beyond that which is available in more pleasant surrounds, and finally ascends—but only for a while. Persephone (and her initiate) must accept the cycles that will inevitably change her circumstance, for better or for worse, and not allow the shadow of Hades to hang over and inhibit her while she is above ground. Likewise, she must concentrate on her duties as Queen of the Dead when she is in that role: daydreaming about picking flowers would be detrimental if she neglected her subterranean tasks.

In addition, Persephone finds some pleasure and even love in the underworld. In one version of the myth, she is joined there by the beautiful Adonis when he is killed by a wild boar and ends up sharing him for half the year with Aphrodite, enjoying his presence for a great deal of her time in the chthonic realms. This symbolizes the possibility of joy even within compromising circumstances. Such pleasure within adversity of course demands a particularly philosophical overview, an acceptance of her lot in its entirety. Only in this way can Persephone find peace of mind. Similarly must every being adapt to their situation, however temporarily, and work with rather than against the facts in order to render improvement and change. This encompasses the aspects that are basically unchangeable; the features of our lives that maybe for the sake of others, or perhaps through practical impossibility, we cannot alter, such as health issues, our relatives, birth status, and so on.

Persephone also indicates the need for balance, for working knowledge of both outer and inner realms. Worldly sophistication is nothing if not balanced by spirituality and the capacity of renunciation; likewise, in order to live successfully in both domains, it is necessary to abide in society and to understand to some extent the minds of others. Many ascetics provide services of incalculable value to mankind, from a solitary Himalayan cave or a temple temenos; however, this yogic strain and capacity is rarely (if ever) found in the West. Our reality dictates that a foot in both worlds is usually the most balanced and progressive route to liberation. This is the equipoise that Persephone perfectly exhibits.

Overcoming Regret and Depression: Preparation

The psychological archetype or blueprint represented by the character of Persephone is of particular relevance to those who feel their mood swings and depressive urges are beyond their control, and whose minds are bending under the conviction that they are "going insane." Symptoms particular to this deity include symbolic dreams, presentiments and attention to omens or auguries; menstrual and hormonal highs and lows. For those who feel that their objective circumstances are the root cause of their despond and who are looking for a lighter form of self-healing, Saraswati (spiritual/creative) or Lakshmi (physical/material) are recommended in lieu of Persephone.

In Persephone, outer circumstances provide a metaphor for internal reality. The negative aspects of one's life: ill health, arguments, or charmless surrounds, reflect the inner reality: grief, regret, or depression. Likewise, positive or neutral traits are paralleled on the physical plane. Her mindset is the key to self-transformation, and it is with this knowledge we approach Persephone, the astral/causal analogue of our own condition.

Although the most pernicious form of regret is self-blame, there are many shades of anguish in Hades, several of the "what if" or "if only" ilk. We can drive ourselves to distraction with conjecture and the "grass is always greener" conviction that an alternative life-route would have been more rewarding, loving, prestigious, and so on; especially if our personal choices have led to tragedy. This may take any form; it is our own interpretation of the situation that makes it so. Consequently, one is left feeling bereft, often too intimidated by more potential suffering to make further life decisions.

How can this paralysis be cured? Persephone can help remedy it by raising our consciousness above the ephemeral and helping us see that all probability levels contain this same lesson in one form or another. The process, however painful, has been necessary for individual soul-development; and, more fatalistically, *this* is the life we were "meant" to lead. These and lateral thought processes are a suitable preamble to the Persephone visualizations but are not to be perceived as excuses. Meditation on the Higher Self and its all-pervasive influence on our lives, however obfuscated by trivia and disbelief, will be highly beneficial prior to approaching Persephone.

A ritual bath is not necessary, nor is internal calmness and serenity. Persephone is best approached when one is feeling intense. Lunar herbs such as rosemary and mint may be helpful in evoking this goddess's presence in your psyche, but basically all you require is your confusion, misery, and imagination.

Visualization for Overcoming Regret and Depression

Take a few deep breaths and think of the experience you wish to transform as existing in the underworld. Envision it literally underground, and yourself inside it; in a dark labyrinthine prison if the problem is complicated; in a simple but scary maze if it is less so. Fill it with the symbols of your circumstance. For example, people whose input influenced the situation might be represented by masks or pictures on the wall, and you might be wearing something indicative of your state of being when the crisis hit.

Walk around your previous life. Try to feel the same emotions, desires, and concerns you had then, and to think the same thoughts. If you have always felt this way, then imagine your present circumstances as existing underground, surrounded by the symbolic paraphernalia relevant to your depression.

If this process causes you pain, imagine the pain as arrows shot into you as if you were quarry; pluck them out and keep them in a bundle in your hand.

It is good to physically enact pulling out the arrows. Make sure you have them all.

Now, recall the moment the crisis hit. If there is no specific time, pick a happy memory and focus on that instead. Then remember how you found yourself plummeting into the chthonic chaos of the underworld; grappling for a hold but finding none; falling lost through inner space. You had been caught in a net; a trap. For a moment all points of reference were lost—there was just the sensation of accelerating descent. Then, with a shuddering crash, you landed in the scene of your present circumstances in the underworld.

Here you are, still caught in the snare.

Look down at your body, still tangled in the netting. To get anywhere, you are first going to have to break through this spider's web of misfortune. So: cut or tear yourself out of the net. Remember, this latticework represents the circumstances that brought you here, and its strength and consistency will reflect this. Take as long as you need to get out of the net. When you do, bundle it up and keep it with the arrows.

Now sit up and look around. Lonely and afraid, you see the shadows flickering like dark flames on the lofty walls around you; your movements echo eerily in the cavernous chambers. Spend a couple of moments really feeling your vulnerability and fear. Then clutch your net and arrows and look around for something or someone to help you. You feel like a child who is without its mother for the first time. Everything seems vast and full of potential danger. You long for some protection or comfort, but your only source is far, far away. The icons in your chamber are mute, immobile. Your gaze flicks frantically across the walls and corridors of glowering darkness, seeking some relief.

As it does, you notice an eerie light coming from your left. The silvery luminescence gradually brightens the scene; in fact, isn't that a path at your feet?

Looking closer, still holding the net and arrows as if they were a talisman, you see that you are standing on a black-and-white tiled and winding pavement that actually feels vibrant through the soles of your feet. Pulsating there, tingling up your body to your spine, it seems as if it might lead somewhere redemptive. You have little to lose—there is nothing for you here

Persephone

now—so you decide to trace the palely illuminated path to its source. As you walk, you move deeper into the heart of Hades.

The air here smells musty and heavily recycled, and it sits like a dusty blanket on your chest. You begin to long for something fresher and more wholesome. You quicken your pace.

Soon there is nothing left to see but the bleak, barren slopes of the imprisoning walls and the black and white checkered tiles of the marble floor. You are a solitary chess piece in an abandoned game. This place is forsaken of the gods, an area few consciousnesses would choose to visit. You begin to wish you had stayed in the little corner of Hades which you knew—at least it held symbols you recognized and reminded you of home.

With one fingertip you nervously caress an arrow-point, barely aware of your body. You are watching the path become a wider floor, suggestive of some kind of portal. It takes you just a few more steps to reach a black pillar to the left and a white to the right. Between them, the light is strong. You continue to move toward it.

At the center of the refulgence is revealed the figure of a cloaked and veiled woman. She sits upon an impressive stone throne, elaborately carved with figures of mythological beasts, three-headed dogs, and crowds awaiting passage across the treacherous river Styx. Skulls adorn the armrests.

The queenly form glows like a full moon in the dark; her incongruously sky-blue eyes shine through the thin veil and regard you. The long tresses that frame the thin but pleasing face are so black they look as if they have been cut out of the air to reveal the void behind light. Her garments are white and blue; rather drab. Her thin lips are smiling slightly but she says not a word. She observes you in tacit nonchalance, though she does not seem unkind. In her hands she holds a voluminous rolled-up scroll of thick vellum. You get a tantalizing glimpse of the mysterious script that embellishes it, but nothing more.

Not wishing to be intrusive or rude, you realize that you must introduce yourself to the luminous goddess you now realize is Persephone. You must present your case to her possible grace.

You kneel before her, place your bundle on the floor in front of you, raise your hands prayerfully, and request her help.

❧

Chapter 12

Explain in your own words or manner how you have accidentally fallen into the underworld from above; how you do not feel it is your time to be here—you want to be free, but something keeps dragging you down. This accidental placement happened after the particular crisis (describe it if you wish); thus you would very much appreciate Persephone's help in restoring you to your preincident peace of mind.

The Queen of the Dead nods awhile, half indicative of comprehension, half of empathy. Recognition of your circumstance registers on her face, which is beginning to show compassion now.

You realize she is thinking that she too would like to return above ground but cannot. Her bright blue eyes convey an acute telepathy. Before you know it, you the supplicant and Persephone the deity become involved in a silent conversation.

Explain to her what you have learned from your "fall" and the time you have spent in the underworld but now you would like to return to the realms of the living in order to express and use your newfound life skills. Invest this statement with belief and enthusiasm. The greater your conviction, the more likely Persephone is to help you.

The problem is, of course, that you still feel encumbered by the emotions and situations engendered by the circumstance that propelled you down here in the first place.

Your eyes fall on your arrows and net. Persephone follows your gaze and smiles. Still without a word, she unrolls the vellum and hands you a quill. You instinctively understand that you are to write down your feelings and hurts, the things that are holding back your progress; you are to perform a thorough catharsis that Persephone will then guard for you along with the bundles of arrows and net.

Really let yourself go with the writing. If possible, physically write things down as you envision your writing material being Persephone's vellum and quill. Be as honest and purgative as you possibly can. Let it all out. Spend as long as you need in this process.

When you have finished, Persephone will roll the scroll up tight again. If you have physically committed your angst to paper, roll that up too. You will not look at it again. At the end of the exercise you will burn or bury it.

❀

Persephone

Persephone also takes the arrows and net into her safekeeping. She is effectively removing the causes of pain that have led you to this untimely descent into the underworld.

She hands you a burning torch. As you thank her, be aware of the wisdom you have accrued during your time in Hades and in her divine presence. This is the only reciprocal gift Persephone really requires.

Persephone inclines her head, and you instantly ascend.

With the torch lighting your Persephone-propelled way, you arrive at the same scene from which you began your journey, only now it is imbued with fresh air and light. See your friends and family walking about here, looking animated and brighter than the gloomy masks you envisioned before. Feel yourself in your new role as light-bearer where previously you were the raven of doom.

You know that if you fall again, you will be able to enlist the goddess's help once more and that your appreciation of the world of the living will be all the stronger for having been denied it a while.

Breathe the luminescence of your new lease on life and fill your lungs with the bright prana of pleasure and potential. Keep inhaling and exhaling this light until your whole body is as aglow with golden refulgence as Persephone's was with silver energy.

When you are imbued with solar light in every pore, a positive sun deity yourself, it is time to open your eyes.

CHAPTER 13

HECATE

It has been a prosperous month for Corinna and her husband. Their olive groves have flourished in the clement weather and Corinna's stomach is swelling like a fruit with another ripening child. Their two sons and daughter are growing up strong and bright. As the moon has reached her fullness, so too have their fortunes waxed.

Carefully she prepares her gifts of bread, wine, wild bee's honey, and corn cakes. Into each of these she invests a portion of her own essence, willing a thank you to the Goddess of Bad Fortune for keeping away, and a request for a healthy pregnancy and easy birth when the time is right. The midwife who roots among the herbs at night knows how to deliver a blessed child.

In her cocoon of light, she makes ready these offerings, the unnerving feeling of being watched only slightly counteracted by the warmth of the oven and the wholesome smell of fresh bread. Outside, the night descends like a slowly settling murder of crows.

When her preparations are complete, Corinna ensures that the children are safe in their beds and leaves the villa to her husband's watchful eye. She takes her gifts wrapped in fresh white linen spun by her own hand at the dark of the moon, lights a torch, and leashes black dogs from the yard.

She is methodical in her actions, attempting with practical concerns to eradicate a little of the sensation of a set of beady eyes on her, but Hecate is strong tonight—she easily outweighs Corinna's sanity. Strange thoughts rise unbidden in her mind, as they always do when she makes this journey. Moods infest her blood and storm the flimsy barricades of reason; she dwells on what might have been, on the soul of her unborn child; she dreams of the underworld, of other lives.

Barefoot, she makes her way toward the crossroads, one league away. A chill breeze makes the hair on her arms rise; she wraps her thin shawl closer to her skin.

Except for the light thud of her feet on the deserted path, her breathing, and the dog's eager panting, all is quiet. No noise disturbs the silence of the pines, their bristling darkness flanking her on both sides. Animals hold their breath as the fire-lit woman and her dog make their winding pilgrimage through the dark woods.

Eventually, Corinna reaches the crossroads. A triple-headed stake marks the place, fashioned with the body of a snake from which a mare, dog, and lion glare. Silently, she kneels and calls to Hecate. She leaves her sacrifice.

Chapter 13

As she hears the woman's footsteps receding, a luridly painted child emerges from the bushes. Her rumbling stomach reminds her of her real mission here. She gathers the foodstuffs, and those left by Hecate's other pilgrims, with grateful haste. She will share it with some of the others. She has not tasted good wine for a month now— though she often smells it on men's breath. This offertory flagon will be a special treat.

Hecate, all beak and talon, watches from the tree.

The next time she sees Corinna, it will be in the presence of the blood of life.

OF ALL THE GODDESSES to have exploded into popular consciousness in the twenty years since this book was originally scribed, Hecate is foremost. She has been conjured from the shadows to be studied in depth as spiritual guide and as primary deity; international groups have amalgamated in her name and under her aegis. Festivals and events are again held in her honor. Numerous books have been written on Hecate both from a personal and academic standpoint.

It seems only right that this mysterious figure should feature in latter-day popular imagination, emerging from the liminal zone at the borders of consciousness as the esoteric becomes less so and what was once occult is increasingly revealed. To Hecate are again attributed honors more akin to those originally her own, which according to Hesiod were many and varied.

In *The Theogony* we are told that Hecate's powers include donning (or denying) agricultural fertility; bestowing wealth in return for sacrifices and prayers; blessing equestrians, games contestants, and fishermen; and nursing the young. She is said to be the only child of Perses with Leto's sister Asteria, and as such is cousin to the lofty Artemis and Apollo. Furthermore, Hecate is described as "she whom Zeus the son of Kronos honored above all." That the king of the gods is deemed to hold Hecate in such high esteem underlines the key role she played in the Hellenistic pantheon of the sixth century BCE and earlier. We are told that Zeus gave her splendid gifts, and a share of the earth and ocean. Hesiod states that "she received honour also in starry heaven, and is honored exceedingly by the deathless gods."

Hecate

In the Homeric hymn to Demeter, it is "Hecate of the shining head-tire, as she was thinking delicate thoughts" who hears Kore's cries for help as she is abducted and who brings news of the horror to Demeter. Brandishing her flaming torches, Hecate aids the distraught mother in the search for the maiden. In due course it is "Hecate of the fair wimple" who joins Kore-Persephone in gloomy Erebus for the third of the year she must spend with her husband, serving as "her queenly comrade and handmaiden."

We see from these brief examples that Hecate is historically a goddess of many facets. She is variously described as a three-faced lunar goddess presiding deity of ghosts and the Dark Arts; a great Earth-Mother; a magickally skilled underworld psychopomp, Queen of the Dead; and even World Savior, amongst other manifestations. As well as being honored at gateways and doors to both homes and cities as guardian against evil spirits, Hecate famously presides over crossroads, particularly ones involving a triumvirate of routes.

Hecate's indubitable skills as a sorceress make her capable of being any and all of the above; indeed, it seems that she inhabits the form best suited to the aspect she is currently displaying. In autumn she may manifest in the mind's eye as a wily older lady wrapped in a billowing cloak; during festivals or sabbats she may choose to appear in her younger-looking or three-headed form. To those excited by the power she represents—maybe a little glamoured by it—Hecate may seem mesmerizing, perhaps overtly sexual, and creatively fructifying. As with all deities, her presence is marked more by atmosphere and wavelength than appearance.

Whatever her manifestation or phase, the ancient goddess Hecate is intimately associated with the moon, magick, and witchcraft, and she is Mistress of the Night. She is said to ride the dark night skies in her lunar chariot, her starfire torch burning with an icy, supernatural light, confirming her mastery of land, sea, air, and fire. In her triform manifestation, her three faces represent, amongst other things, the three major stages of the lunar cycle: new, full, and dark (or new, half and full), and though she was sometimes worshipped on the morning of a new moon, as Queen of Sorcery she is also associated with and worshipped during the dark phase. She can look in every direction simultaneously. These stages have been popularly paralleled with feminine development, their correspondences being maiden (Kore), mother (Demeter), and crone (Hecate), respectively, colluding with the Elizabethan concept of Hecate as aged hag, though in fact it is her wisdom, not her image that make her so. The synchronicity of the menstrual cycle with the lunar month has always been recognized, and in her lunar aspect Hecate presides over menstruation, as over childbirth and menopause.

The essence of this deity is as untenable as moonlight; she often manifests as intuition, dreams, and symbolic experiences. As with several goddesses, one translation of her name is "She Who Works From Afar." It is said that only dogs can sense Hecate's whereabouts; they were sacred to her and used as sacrificial offerings, especially black ones; often these dogs were designated carriers of the Grecian "miasma," the impurities of the community or individual, and slaughtered in much the same way as the scapegoat. Hecate thus conferred magickal purity. Dog meat was sometimes eaten in her honor. One of her signature birds is the owl; bats and black birds are also amongst her entourage, as are other creatures of the night and those associated with sorcery. The 1795 painting *Triple Hecate* by William Blake, since entitled *The Night of Enitharmon's Joy*, beautifully depicts Hecate half naked, half clothed in darkness, reading from a grimoire, surrounded by creatures whose strength and mystique, like her own, considerably exceed their beauty. Unconventional, black-haired and as pervasive as the darkness itself, *Hecate Pharmakea* is associated with mandrake and other powerful plants and herbs, often the toxic ones. She is the supreme witch, the sorceress extraordinaire without whose presence no coven is complete.

Needless to say, it is ideal to channel your own invocations during ritual, allowing the Divine, your subconscious and the magick of the moment to meld uniquely. Recital, however, is sometimes a better structure, particularly in groups where pressure to "perform" may be an inhibiting issue. At the Glastonbury Hekate Conference of 2014, for example, British witch Melissa Harrington shared a spellbinding Hecate invocation of her own, spontaneously transmitted to and by her in Wookey Hole caves in Somerset, a superlatively bat-heavy and subterranean venue for such an evocation. See the bibliography and recommended sources for a link: it's worth a listen.

Hecate

One of the most important aspects of magickal training is challenging the neophyte's beliefs, and particularly their prejudices. Within witchcraft, the domain in which Hecate reigns, a deliberate attempt is made to reclaim taboo areas of the psyche and, indeed, to revel in them as a counterreaction to their previous suppression. This includes three of the most powerful forces in our lives: social mores, sex, and death. The concept of the witch's sabbat and its lateral manifestations was for many centuries an orgiastic, atavistic replay of fertility rites, Pan worship, and the Roman Saturnalia that Christian church-inspired neuroses only heightened. The idea was not just to revive the Pagan gods, but to regain conscious control of the primal faculties and harness their profound effects on our lives. These goals remain today, though the mode of attaining them may have changed somewhat. The artist and occultist Austin Osman Spare perhaps best epitomized this aspect of the occult and Hecate's place in it (from his personal standpoint) through his relationship with his patron, Mrs. Paterson, and the rituals, sigils, and drawings that ensued. His obsession with the witch-crone and her hideous-seeming, beguiling sexuality took the concept of being hag-ridden to a suitably challenging and liberal degree.

The chaotic, "sinister," and seemingly negative side of our psyches has its place. As patroness of prostitutes, thieves, beggars, and pariahs, Hecate protects those on the outskirts of society. She spreads her voluminous cloak around the feared and hated, the outcasts and "inferior." She represents the objective eye searing through the elaborate façade of standard society. Riches and education cannot deceive her; she views the heart. When this heart is a little nibbled by the worms of misfortune, she proffers a healing vial. Hecate does not judge, except on respect extended in her direction. To those who lack the emotional intelligence necessary to encompass her, she will seem the most terrifying of harridans.

Being the epitome of magickal knowledge and thus often manifesting as older and wiser, and certainly Other, Hecate at times inspires the repulsion felt particularly in the modern West for physical frailty and the subsequent threat of death. Modern society has become one in which cosmetic surgery is touted as the necessary alternative to the visible experience of the life-adept: thought-lines, wrinkles and crow's feet; a hierarchy in which the tradition of

166

❀

tribal ancients is so overruled by youth culture that some elderly communities do indeed seem to have become empty vessels. If one is perceived as nothing, it can be very difficult to maintain a sense of something. For the marginalized aged, Hecate can prove a feisty anti-boredom serum and a powerful elixir of lust for life, often manifesting as active intelligence.

This archetypal spiritual sorceress and queen of all witches, champion of the outcast and vaunter of the unpalatable, can make or break masks at will. She is generous in offering third chances when others stall at a second. Hecate is the metaphorical bearded lady—matron of untouchables, bringer of creative challenge. No therapy can shake this divine devil from our back, for she is the part of us that is perennially unacceptable. She is the counterreaction to all insecurities; the part of the psyche that rebels against feeling outcast. The cause could be anything from physical appearance—too fat, too bald, the "wrong" race—to gender dysphoria, unconventional sexuality, or the harboring of unpopular convictions (for example, being a Pagan in a Catholic school), to the ages-old inferiority complex. Regarding Hecate and transsexuality, Walter Burkert states in *Greek Religion: Archaic and Classical*: "Castrated priests are attested in the cult of Kubaba-Kybele, and *Hecate of Lagina* in Caria also has eunuchs, just as Aphrodite-Astarte has her male transvestites," underlining a link between Hecate and liminal sexualities. However, classical scholar Dr. James Rietveld says of this: "Lagina is a strange site with that particular Hecate connecting more to the Carian-Luwian goddess so it is difficult to make her characteristic of Hecate as a whole." Whether this connection with transvestitism and transsexuality is explicit or implicit, it is certain that Hecate will respond to the prayers and sacrifices of those like her, who exist primarily in peripheral zones.

Hecate's traditional guardianship of crossroads demonstrates her presiding over life-changing decisions. As *Hecate Kleidouchos* her primary symbol is the key, she as a doorway to both inner and outer mysteries, new phases of life cycle, an understanding of life's transience. As well as crafty midwife to gods and mortals, Hecate is a succoring shadow at death. The Homeric hymn to Hecate refers to her as "tender-hearted" in respect for her role as psychopomp and aider of Persephone.

The importance of Hecate in the Eleusinian Mysteries is underlined by her additional role as protector of the harvest, one of her festivals falling around that time. Under her aegis the crops are kept from blight, and travelers from harm: she was propitiated to aid journeys through wild and dangerous places.

Hecate may be protector of outcasts, but her reign is supreme in her own domain. In her, we find all the wisdom and capability that shamanic cultures attribute to age; a sublime transcendence of worldly concerns. She does not discriminate between those in a fortunate life cycle and those whose karma holds them at the bottom of the Wheel of Fortune. As guardian of the latter, she renders sacred the profane and befriends the pariah. Consequently, the Hecate godform can help lance the fear behind prejudice (often disguised behind a curtain of sanctimony) and bring cosmic balance into situations of discrimination.

As well as acting as cosmic equalizer, the presence of Hecate enlivens powerful magickal currents and declares the omnipotence of the soul. A variety of personae, magickal and psychological, become available to us when Hecate is near. Past incarnations, or nomadic archetypal personalities, may come to the fore for the purposes of exploration. Psychism becomes pronounced. Inner development and increased occult awareness are inevitable in Hecate's presence, but the road may not be easy. Hecate, being the dark and wily aspect of the triad, is unlikely to pick for us the simplest route at the crossroads, but rather, the one that will challenge us to the fullness of our capacity. Mediumistic and wise she certainly is, but she'll give her devotees a run for their lives.

The flipside of Hecate's gift of profound wisdom is the ever-tricky threat of egoism. Hecate may be the queen of all witches, but all too often one finds her mundane archetypes making the same claim. Beware such hubris! Like Spirit itself, Hecate's blessings and powers are available to all, never confined to one person or group of people. Traits may vary in strength, certainly, just as the individual unfolds in many stages of development—child, adult, and post-incarnation—and is never quite the same twice. Seen through Hecate's egalitarian eyes, all godforms and spiritual paths are different but equal, and all beings great and small are equally divine. The difference is only in the manifestation.

Encountering Hecate

A good time to contact Hecate is any major sabbat (see glossary), particularly Samhain, the winter equinox, or at one of the modern dates dedicated to her. Working with a moon appropriate to your intent goes without saying for any witch. However, all godforms are available at all times if a suitable mental environment is created for them to inhabit. In Hecate's case, a strong awareness of the seasons as reflected in nature will help. Feeling darkly emotional and hormonal seems to add an extra impetus to the proceedings in my own experience.

Concentrate on this beautiful dark goddess, cloaked in mystery, one eye seeming to pierce your soul from her darksome visage. She may manifest as triple-headed, as old and wise, or as ineffably young and beautiful: whatever the case, she demands respect, and you instinctively give it.

She is surrounded by her colors: purple, mauve, black, and sometimes green. Candles of these shades of darkness and rebirth will help evoke the goddess.

There are some excellent Hecate incenses (and recipes) available if you are looking to create a ritualistic atmosphere to enhance your visualization and spellworking. Storax, myrrh, and bay leaves are cornerstones. Kyphi works well too.

A walk in nature, perhaps in an overgrown cemetery on an atmospheric day, or at twilight or by moonlight, is another suitable preamble to channeling Hecate. Pay attention to the trees, flora, and fauna, feeling the life currents flowing through the elements, manifesting in people and patterns of humanity everywhere. Feel the mystery behind it; the power of the dead and the ancestors, and the cosmic intelligence that directs all growth and decline. Hecate lives in the magic behind the veil, and her presence gives depth to shadows, highlights the luster of red and green leaves, bestows life with a tingle of anticipation, and causes candlelight to become entrancing; a flaming torch leading us to new astral worlds.

Exercise for Overcoming Prejudice

For Hecate as Mistress of Magick, it seems particularly apt that readers should create their own visualization. However, as it can be difficult to work without structure, I have provided a skeleton. As ever, readers are encouraged to adjust the details to suit their purpose.

It goes without saying that those in a hostile environment will benefit from psychic self-protection. One of my own favorites for such situations is imagining the body moving within an inviolable pillar of violet flame. This has the effect of cooling down the emotional responses of others and of oneself if provoked. It makes the perpetuator less visible by muting their lower vibrations and heightening their spiritual presence. There are numerous such techniques, pretty much something for every occasion. Particularly recommended is *The Witch's Shield: Protection Magick and Psychic Self-Defense* by Christopher Penczak (Llewellyn Worldwide, 2010).

However, in situations of great enmity or in which a favorable response is required from another party, a little bit of perspective bending may be required so that one's idiosyncrasies seem interesting rather than alienating … or even better, relatable. You might think it's a tall order, but as you will discover, all you have to do is concentrate your willpower and ask.

Walk outside until you feel attuned as mentioned in the preparations section. Amazingly, the park nearest to me at the time I originally scribed this spell had a statue of Hecate at its gate; in Victorian times it had been a botanical garden of some standing, and the four seasons were represented as statues at the entrance. Hecate was featured in her once-popular concept as wily old hag, an artistic rendition of the Greek goddess accurate in its conveying of great wisdom, if not of her purported original form; here, she represented winter, difficult times, and the pariah. This was an obvious pilgrimage point, and visiting helped me align with relevant aspects of the goddess. I also concentrated on the crone and her symbols and colors, and I imagined her walking through the park, scattering autumn leaves on the breeze as she passed on her way to the underworld to visit Persephone. Use your own environment to stoke your imagination: the most important part is the attunement to Hecate and the magickal wavelength.

If the moon is waning, you will be correlating this with the waning of the resistance of your opponents. If waxing, the focus will be on your increasing strength, attractive qualities and acceptance in the group whose enmity you wish to quell.

For the visualization itself, use a small candle to represent the resistance and negativity toward you, and a flat symbol such as a pentacle pendant to stand for your beliefs, idiosyncrasies, and essence. Try to use whatever feels most apt: if someone is giving you a hard time because they are jealous of you, try burning a small green candle to diminish their venom; if the harassment is racial, use a symbol of your culture or background to embed in the melting wax of their waning hostility. An obvious psychological approach is to maintain an efficient, friendly front (make sure not to come across as desperate, vulnerable or too willing to please): your opponents will try to undermine it, but eventually your courage will be respected, if not liked.

Place the candle on top of or right beside the emblem so that any falling wax will melt onto it. Then strongly visualize each person concerned in turn (or *en masse* if it is a group unknown to you), and mentally transfer their feelings of antipathy into the candle. Once you feel that the candle is imbued with every ounce of negativity they feel for you, ask for Hecate's aid and light it.

As the candle burns, envision their resistance, fear, and hostility being burned away; as the wax melts onto your symbol, imagine them embracing the essence they have previously resisted, becoming as pliant as warm wax in its presence.

Call to Hecate and ask for her aid in your endeavor. Visualize her coming to you in the form you most prefer (or wait and see how she chooses to manifest to you—it could be revealing). Feel your body being invested with the beauty, strength, and sorcerous cunning of this dark goddess. Feel her knowledge and wisdom permeating you; know that you are blessed no matter what the conventional, consensus reality of the maya-matrix might have to say about you.

Do this visualization for however long you feel you can maintain a high level of concentrated attention. Five minutes for three consecutive days at the same time is always a good amount, as a start.

With the blessings of the Goddess, your differences should become irrelevant and you ought to find common ground not reliant on social or intellectual similarities (or at the very least, mutual tolerance with a dash of empathy). Hecate will topple the petty hierarchy and provide a situation in which mutual respect is of benefit to all.

CHAPTER 14

APHRODITE

She hypnotizes, like the sea.

Waves of euphoria inebriate the senses when she is near; I stand on a rocky outcrop of reason, watching, the vertiginous impulse compelling me to jump. To be consumed in a rapture of water, drowned in the salty brew that looks pure but promises not to be.

Desiring amnesia, my impulses refuse analysis. I feel myself being drawn further into her enchantment, colluding; will under glamour. Ambrosia is offered from a golden chalice, and I drink it greedily. Languor settles on the brain like an eternity of silken sheets.

She performs her part with éclat, feeding off my balmy smile. I am as helpless as a love-stricken adolescent. She lets me paddle in her essence, then withdraws the tide; but I will get her and haul her inland.

Later she will lie on her back on the fallow furrows, her eyes sky-blue and reflective, her face a golden glow—haughty yet vulnerable; an invitation to be conquered. So, I will plow her into the earth, commit her life-blood to the soil, and attempt to immobilize her so she does not do this to me again. She always will, of course.

I cannot believe I think this way when she is near. And yet, she makes me. She knows what she is doing. Or does she?

She notices me brooding and brings her scent a little closer … she touches me.

I forget I ever had a rational thought.

ACCORDING TO HESIOD, APHRODITE was created when Ouranos's castrated genitals were cast into the sea. Just as Athene's birth from Zeus's head affirms her mental prowess, Aphrodite's creation from sea-frothing genitalia reveals her as the embodiment of sexual desire. As such, she is a deity of unrivaled popularity. As the legend of Paris's judgment amply demonstrates, the gifts of Artemis (independence, hunting skills, athleticism) and Hera (power, glory, prestige) can barely compete. Indeed, all other goddesses fade in comparison to this epitome of human and celestial desire.

When a person is *in aphrodite*, entranced by love or lust, reason can never prevail. Moreover, those who attempt to avoid Aphrodite and refuse her gifts do so at their own peril. Hippolytus, for example, dedicated himself to Artemis and scorned Aphrodite; in anger, the latter caused his stepmother, Phaedra, to fall in love with him. Unable to bear rejection, Phaedra then accused him of rape. The long chain of revenge did not end until Hippolytus was dead and the family horribly shamed. The highly morally questionable mythic message is loud and clear: to deny the flow of one's libido, personified by Aphrodite, or to live in, but not comply with, normal society is to court disaster. But Aphrodite and morality rarely go hand in hand.

It is, therefore, fitting that the Minotaur, symbolic of sexuality so suppressed that it has become a raging subconscious beast, should be a tool of her vengeances. Incest and bestiality are among the punishments inflicted by Aphrodite on those who deny the natural outlets of their sexuality and thereby refuse to do her homage. These are surprising traits indeed to find in one of such pleasing looks and golden mien. Yet it is Aphrodite's dynamism, both in its positive and negative aspects, that saves her from the category of mere ornamentation. She is as beneficent as she is malicious, as intense as she is fickle, as physically beautiful as she is sickening. Aphrodite brings the affliction of love, the wound whose fevered visions are its own redemption; for only by living through it can the victim, probably willing but a victim nonetheless, really be cured.

These apparent contradictions have produced one of the most enduring of ancient goddesses, an archetype and name instantly recognizable to the modern world. It is typical of the ancient Greek mindset that Aphrodite is not like, say, Lilith in Judeo-Christian mythology, downright defamed for her powerful sexuality; Aphrodite emerges as a dualistic being with good and bad points, just like the human psyche itself. The rational culture of ancient Greece produced godforms of reflective dualistic ilk.

Aphrodite is out to get what she can while she can, and her archetype is present in many women today. Having witnessed the abominable abuse of the chthonic form of femininity that predated her, she has become the teenage daughter with all of the power and none of the generosity of her mother. Her role as fertility goddess does remain, but in a new form. Aphrodite's ability to engender growth resembles that of a solar deity in lieu of the comfortable earth mother, a comparison underlined by her popular epithet, "the Golden," and by her association with birds and empyrean qualities. She brings about sexual feeling of all types, not just procreative. Her worshippers are free to revel in amorous sensations of any nature, and the works of ancient poets such as Catullus and Sappho do her appropriate homage. Aphrodite's sexuality has become her own rather than a free-for-all, but she maintains the ability to stimulate proliferation in plants, animals, humans and, indeed, gods.

As a muse, Aphrodite is unrivaled: look at how much art, music, poetry and culture harps on and/or was created by sexual and amorous desire! It accounts for the vast majority of human creativity. Childbirth is painful and dangerous, as indeed are childhood and parenthood, so basic sexual pleasure has been created to ensnare the body into not caring about the consequences. Sexuality is a drug strong enough to perpetuate the human species by temporarily inuring one to all repercussions. Society concurs with and manipulates this "biological necessity" in a million ways, pummeling us with tacky love songs and movies, making out that we cannot be complete without "the one," expecting marriage and children from us, programming the individual to expect to find "it all" in another flawed being, when in fact, only the Divine can provide that truly meaningful connection. However, sexuality and partnership can be "gateway drugs" leading to a full experience of God/dess; for many it is the alchemical mother lode. The human body is almost always invested with this hormonal urge whatever one's orientation and whether or not one wishes or is able to reproduce. Aphrodite can create utter havoc in our lives, or she can lead one to visionary experience of Spirit, as she is well known to those wise ones who have gained control of their kundalini energy.

Needless to say, Aphrodite is therefore a mistress of the arts of self-decoration and seduction. Much attention is given in the Homeric hymn to Aphrodite and her jewelry: "a well-wrought crown…earrings of orichalcum and of precious gold…her delicate neck and white bosom adorned with chains of gold wherewith are bedecked the golden-snooded Hours themselves." The Andrew Lang translation uses some wonderfully descriptive verbs such as "she prinked" to describe Aphrodite at her toilette. Indeed, the only ones who can hope to avoid falling for Aphrodite's erotic arts are Artemis, homely Hestia, and their devotees: "But of all others there is none, of blessed gods or mortal men, that hath escaped Aphrodite."

Zeus himself has been shamed by Aphrodite, who "hath lightly laid him in the arms of mortal women, Hera not wotting it." Gods should never descend to the level of mortals, particularly those already married to a goddess, but Aphrodite's allure is so great that she can cause the King of Olympia himself to lust helplessly after the human form. In revenge, Zeus makes Aphrodite fall in love with the mortal Anchises, another taboo union. Despite her disguising herself as an ordinary human, Anchises recognizes the goddess by "her height, her beauty, and glistering raiment...for she was clad in a vesture more shining than the flame of fire, and with twisted armlets and glistering earrings flower-fashion." There is no concealing the divine beauty that is Aphrodite! Yet still this "laughter-loving" goddess tricks the beau into accepting her in love—he "loosened her girdle" and that was that.

Upon awaking, Anchises beholds her in her fully immortal beauty and is simultaneously terrified and smitten. Knowing that his ordinary life will not be worth living now that he has experienced the love of a goddess, he begs her to "suffer me not to live a strengthless shadow among men." Aphrodite cannot grant him immortality without him aging perpetually and undergoing the same fate as poor old Tithonus, who suffers eternal life without eternal youth thanks to his affair with Aurora—and the Greek gods detest frailty. Instead, Aphrodite bears him a son, Aeneas, consoling Anchises with the fact that through his seed, his bloodline will receive great honors as heroes of Troy. However, she insists that Anchises lie about it and claim that his son was mothered on a nymph, thus protecting her reputation as a goddess, and again displaying her cunning and manipulative aspects.

On a psychological level, Aphrodite offers to break the mold of mundane existence and shake the foundations of her lovers with a sublime as well as physical passion. "It is better to have loved and lost, than to never have loved at all" is a motto the goddess herself might well have written. She is also all about the thrill of the chase and the gratification of desire, however unwise it might be. Even the animals "couple two by two in the shadowy dells" at the very sight of her, and great is the fertility she brings.

It is appropriate that the goddess of love is frequently coupled with Ares, the god of war. Just as earth itself spins between the planets Venus and Mars, the terrestrial condition is one of suspension between love and enmity, the two most powerful instincts that pull us here and there according to personal proclivities and the influence exerted by each. Thus, of the four children born to Aphrodite by Ares, two are positive: *Eros*, meaning love, and *Anteros*, meaning reciprocal love; and two negative: *Deimos*, or terror, and *Phobos*, meaning fear. In other versions, Aphrodite presents her lame husband Hephaestus with Deimos and Phobos, though they have in fact been sired by Ares. In revenge,

Aphrodite

her smith-god spouse traps the lovers in a fishing net and displays them before the gods. However, the plan backfires somewhat as Hermes, Dionysus, and Poseidon all realize how much they desire Aphrodite, and later lie with the irresistible goddess. She brings forth many children thanks to the power of her magick girdle, which she on occasion lends to the love-smitten, that they too might satisfy their desire. Hera herself is one such: even a celestial wife needs a touch of Aphrodite to keep her husband from straying.

Aphrodite can bring either sublimation or tragedy. The story of Helen of Troy is perhaps her best-known act of destruction through vanity, in which love and reciprocal love swiftly become enmity and war. The cost in human blood and suffering is vast. *Eris*, or discord, is rarely far behind the scented train of golden Aphrodite.

Despite the chaos she frequently wreaks, Aphrodite herself is a deity of pronounced social sensibilities, in many aspects more a fan of (albeit titillating) courtly love—a psychological and literal burlesque—than downright sex. She endorses physical passion if it is appropriately timed and stylishly conducted, but crudeness offends her; she is, after all, companion and origin of the lovely Graces. Imagine her horror at parenting Priapus, a boy whose phallus was so large that she sent him away to the countryside to be forgotten about, or at least she hoped! Priapus is one symbol of the extremes Aphrodite can provoke.

She is in essence the female counterpart to the lusty horned god but shirks the task. In her independence, Aphrodite has been civilized. She has formed herself out of the rudimentary clay of her mother into a predatory, self-sufficient entity with complete autonomy. A bludgeon-like phallus is both distasteful and dangerous to her, which is why the vengeful Hera gave a priapic appearance to the son of Aphrodite and Dionysus, a punishment for her amorous antics.

The need to dominate underlies the deceptive frivolity of this goddess's "bubbly" nature. She may be as apt to change with the tides as the foam itself, but it is not through giddiness or lack of intelligence that this is so. Aphrodite follows her own desires wherever they may lead, and her hedonism is as relentless as her ire when roused. Cross her (or even bore her), and you've had it. It is thanks to this tenacity that Aphrodite may be approached for purposes not merely superficial. Relationships blessed by this goddess will prove physically as well as psychologically passionate, and metaphorically or literally fertile.

As for finding new partners, few deities could offer a more interesting chase. Seduction is Aphrodite's forté; she is the ultimate witch when it comes to love spells. She does not flinch when the cerebral becomes physical; Aphrodite is a prime role model for the female libido at its most active. Consequently, for claiming or reclaiming one's independent sexuality, Aphrodite is a supremely suitable godform to invoke.

One word of warning: This deity can have serious repercussions on your life. She will invest you with the power to break hearts and ruin as well as create relationships. Other goddesses such as Hathor, Isis, and Iris may be employed to counterbalance her dizzying influence, providing the groundwork for a more permanent state of affairs.

Approaching Aphrodite: Preparation

Try working with a waxing moon, preferably full. Fridays are sacred to Venus and are thus apt for such invocations. An indulgent ritual bath is highly recommended prior to any activity involving Aphrodite or her qualities. The best candles for this goddess are red, dark orange, and pink. Put lots of bubble bath in the water to recall Aphrodite's emergence from the frothing ocean, and a pinch of cleansing, evocative sea salt. The best scents to use are rose, musk, sandalwood, or any perfume that is an erotic stimulant to you.

If you desire, drink wine or mead in the bath, or a fruit juice—all are appropriate to Aphrodite.

If you wish to burn incense or oil, the scents mentioned above are suitable, as are myrrh or cinnamon. Cypress is also sacred to Aphrodite, but the scent may be a little too medicinal for the purpose.

While lolling in the scented waters, imagine that this bath is the preliminary to a much-anticipated date. You are preparing to meet someone you want to impress. If you are already in a relationship, concentrate on the feelings you had when you first met your partner; if not, envision your ideal counterpart. Either way, contemplate the newness of their unexplored mind and body, the qualities that attract you to them, and what they will be like to kiss. Think about how smitten they will be by you, and how alluring you will be.

Music often helps with fantasies of this ilk; play something upbeat that makes you feel good, or anything that has suitable connotations for you.

As you lie in the warm scented water, concentrate on the chakra that lies at the base of the spine at the genitals, and on the one above it at the spleen. Envision the root chakra growing and glowing in red, and the one above it a mini sun wheel of vibrant orange. Do this until you can feel a powerful energy flowing between the two. Be aware of the combination of these forces quickening your blood with anticipation and confidence.

With your potential encounter still in mind, perform all the mini-rituals you would before any important date; wash your hair or shave if you are so inclined; you may want to use a scented moisturizer afterwards. Once you have completed your toilette, having applied any makeup and/or scent you wish to wear, and are feeling alluring, you are ready to invoke Aphrodite.

Visualization for Finding Your Ideal Sexual Partner

First, perform the preparations described above.

Now, make a list of the qualities of your desired partner. You might want to specify first that any incomers be available and single, or happily polyamorous if apt, and that any interaction will be in your mutual best interest.

Think of the physical traits you find attractive: gender (if relevant), approximate height, weight, age, background, for example—and, most importantly, the character traits you wish for in a partner. Will they be creative? Gentle? Assertive? Artistic? Homely? Adventurous? Write each of your specifications on an individual scrap of paper. If you are not sure what form your ideal partner will take, all the better. The fewer specifications you send out, the wider the range of potential "applicants"—though be sure to add the proviso that they must be good for you and make you happy, and vice versa. You probably have a sense of the essence of your ideal counterpart, so concentrate on that if their qualities seem indefinable.

Once you have prepared your list, take a small red candle, preferably one that is the same color throughout instead of painted on the outside, and dip your fingers into a little scented oil such as orange, ylang-ylang, musk, or rosemary—choose a scent that feels right to you.

Hold the candle at the center of its stem and place it on a piece of red or black silk; rub your fingers simultaneously on both ends of the stick so half is stroked only from the center to the wick, and half from the center to the base. As you do this, visualize the type of person you desire being irresistibly magnetized toward you. Feel yourself surrounded by Aphrodite's golden glow, infinitely attractive to those of your choosing, and sense the approach of your desired partner. You are, in effect, "magnetizing" the candle, which will echo and magnify your call in the ether.

As you rub, continue to feel the conviction within yourself that, as the candle burns, your request will indeed be transmitted into the etheric airwaves. Try to invest all your excitement into the candle wax.

Make sure you have your paper snippets in your hand; ask for Aphrodite's blessing, and light the candle. As the wick lends itself to the flame, know that your request has been received on the astral plane.

Envision Aphrodite standing in a golden haze just behind the candle flame. She is the living epitome of all that you deem attractive, and the power of allurement emanates from her in compelling golden waves.

Watch the flame signaling your sexual desire, and feel free to daydream about how wonderful it will be when you experience the result. Mentally collude with Aphrodite as if she were your best friend, sharing your secrets and giggling with you over your schemes.

When you feel ready, pick the quality you consider primary and commit it to the flame (best to use tweezers); ensure that the message it contains gets through. As it burns, watch Aphrodite receive it on the other side of the candle; she takes the specifications of your special order. Shimmering and smiling, she nods her acquiescence.

Continue in this process until all the qualities you require in your partner-to-be have been reconfirmed by you and burned and assimilated by the goddess. When all have gone, extinguish the candle.

Repeat this process at the same time every day until the candle has burned down. If this is not possible and you feel your request is already bound to be

Aphrodite

granted, allow the red candle to burn down before you put it out. Do not leave it unattended, of course.

Now, wait and see who you've conjured up. Most importantly, enjoy yourself and your love-goddess aspect.

Restimulating the Sex Drive

Most people, especially women, find that their libido all but deserts them at some point or another. This can be due to stress, diet, financial problems, hormones, spiritual concerns, or simply boredom. It is very common for women to go off sex once a relationship has been established, especially after childbirth. In a way, Aphrodite deserts them and a necessarily more homely deity steps in.

The following visualization is for those who wish to realign themselves with the sex goddess not for someone else's sake but because they miss the sensual dimension in their lives. Others may prefer to remain asexual/chaste; there is nothing wrong (and arguably, much right) with this. Energies used in sexual interaction are often rerouted and used for other equally (or more) important purposes. This visualization will help you route the energies back into your sexuality, should you wish to employ them there.

Having performed the preparations described earlier, stand naked before a full-length mirror. If this is too cold or you are uncomfortable, dress in something you like that makes you feel attractive.

Now, imagine your entire body glowing golden: a gentle, warm effulgence that radiates from your mind and your heart. As you do this, half-close your eyes and take several slow, deep breaths. As you breathe with your eyes half-shut, visualize the goddess Aphrodite descending in a golden cloud right behind you. Her cloud merges with yours, and as it does, you feel a physical pleasure permeating your skin, along with a knowledge once understood but long-forgotten that your body is, at least in part, your playground.

Notice that Aphrodite wears a girdle around her waist. A vast amount of sexual energy is concentrated in this golden girdle; it is the ultimate saucy lingerie. This is the girdle that Aphrodite lent to Hera to help seduce her disinterested husband, Zeus—it never fails. Ask Aphrodite if you may borrow it.

Now, take a generous amount of the light that flows freely around the goddess, and spin it into your lower chakras. If you perceive any cracks or blocks in these areas, heal the rifts and unclog the chakras; ground any unclean matter by throwing it at the floor or flicking it away with your fingers. It is best to physically enact these processes.

When the lower and intestinal chakras are bright and feel fully stimulated and strong (a vivid red and orange color), you can stop. Do not quit until these parts of your body feel pleasantly charged with bright energy.

When you feel sated, put one hand on the top of your head and the other on your pubic area. This will even out the energies. Then, for just a moment longer, return to charging your two lowest chakras.

When these are bright and feel fully stimulated and strong, thank Aphrodite and bid her farewell, knowing that a part of her ineffable charm remains with you.

Return to normal, repeating the exercise as often as you wish.

Did Aphrodite give you the girdle? If so, the auspices are good for your libido. Be sure to visualize it around your waist when you are in your next sexual scenario. If she denied you this ultimate aphrodisiac, repeat the exercise until she acquiesces, or accept that now simply is not the right time for that very physical wavelength in your life. Either way, remember that if you borrow that golden glow for long enough, as with the contemplation of any trait, symbol or even godform, it will eventually become a part of you.

Aphrodite

CHAPTER 15

IRIS

The Harpies and Iris shared a childhood nest; and so light and love grew up alongside scheming darkness. Triple-headed monsters haunted the pale child day and night, making deformity familiar to her; a matter of no consequence.

Now, free to wander the world, she journeys between dimensions shedding color and understanding in her wake. Seven iridescent rays provide her bridge; she slides through spectrums of glimmering light. She is fluent in the vibration of each, becoming part of any wavelength and disguising herself as a reflected rain-drop, if the gods so will.

She appears aureoled on the lashes of the lamenting, messages of hope her charge, or sometimes those of resignation. Through Iris's intercession, Demeter was commanded to stoicism over the rape of her daughter. The task, though thankless, was necessary; nature shriveled and man and beast perished while the corn goddess mourned. Iris cannot stand by and witness such imbalance.

And so Iris's life is defined as pronouncer of the will of the gods. She listens, she travels, she tells. Sometimes, she mediates of her own volition, for her soul's palette is extensive, made up of black and white and everything between, and she knows the necessity of all.

Habitually, she emanates an arc between extremes, manifesting as the celestial spectrum-bridge.

GREEK GODDESS OF THE rainbow, Iris is a messenger of the gods, bringer of hope and guidance. She is one of the few who can come and go from Erebus and who can cross the sacred river Styx with impunity. She is described in Hesiod's *Theogony* as bearer of sacred Styx-water whenever the gods had to take an oath. Untruth on their part will result in a year-long co-matose sleep induced by the draft the goddess proffers.

Iris is employed as Hera's handmaiden and is guardian of clouds and rain. However, her chief function is as intermediary. Along with Hermes, Iris is herald and spokesperson for the gods. Traveling by the arc of her rainbow, she bridges the worlds. It is Iris who is sent by Hera to the soporific chambers of Hypnos (Somnus), the god of sleep, to request that dream-visions be sent to certain devoted mortals. Through Iris's intercessions, Hypnos's son, Morpheus, makes known the death of Ceyx to his pining wife, Halcyone. Likewise, in the *Iliad*, Zeus employs Iris as swift dispatcher of urgent messages; a verbal stauncher of blood on the battlefield.

Iris travels with ease and grace between kingdoms and dimensions using her flexible nature to prevent unnecessary suffering. When a mortal is undergoing a slow death, Iris brings relief by severing the silver cord that binds them to their temporary body and thus to this realm. She is a deity of great charity and diplomacy, the antithesis of her sisters, the pestilential Harpies.

When the symbolic champions of spirit, the Boreades, are threatened by the Harpies, Iris is put on the spot. Her positive nature dictates the protection of the Boreades, while her genetic loyalty does not wish for harm to befall her sisters. Those in the dark corner are fighting furiously but slipping under, their venomous spittle flailing in the wind as they shriek and curse. It seems that both parties might come to a sticky end unless Iris compromises her direful sisters by rescuing them. Finally, she corners them into a deal whereby they leave the Boreades and their hapless charge, King Phineus, in peace.

Iris thus mediates between the poles of good and evil, engendering balance amid struggle. Her flexibility and calm in situations that are often dangerous to the outsider are qualities worthy of emulation. It is also interesting that such an active goddess arrests action and, thereby, creates harmony. She is not a mere follower and deliverer of other deities' instructions but is an intelligent and kindly judge in her own right. Iris's overriding qualities are gentle strength and communication skills borne of the art of balance.

As the soft hues of her spectrum suggest, this sweet-natured goddess is a bringer of hope and justice through diplomacy rather than force. Her temperate nature and ability to adapt to a variety of environments, her easy transition between the realms of material life, sleep, and immortality, and her equipoise in matters sacred and profane make Iris a perfect example of spiritual integrity at its most temperate and tactile. She displays the calm, intelligent equilibrium of angelic overview.

Iris can facilitate in a similar manner to Persephone, in that we see how balance is necessary in all things, as is acceptance of change. In Juliet Sharman-Burke's *Mythic Tarot* (highly recommended for those interested in the Greek myths and their practical relevance), Iris is depicted as Temperance, a symbol of self-control even during times of fluctuation. The angel of temperance is the oversoul, anchored by spiritual insight in the ever-changing ocean of physical circumstance. Like Iris, the oversoul exhibits gentle optimism and quiet faith in ultimate good.

❀

Iris

Iris is a guide and a herald, conversant in matters practical as well as spiritual. She is an extremely functional goddess; a bearer of peace to the soul tortured by time and its dead-end facade; her light illuminates the eternity behind it.

Contacting Iris: Preparation

Showering by daylight is a good preliminary to contacting the Iris archetype, perhaps with a crystal in the window, sending shards of spectrum-light about the room.

Snowdrops, flowers in bud, and the symbols of early spring befit this goddess and may help evoke a suitable atmosphere. For those with ethereal proclivities, place a pot of soil in the room to touch if you feel yourself becoming too carried away, or simply stamp on the floor; or make that shower cold. Despite her celestial nature and soaring spirit, Iris keeps both ends of her rainbow firmly planted on the ground.

Initially, you will want to focus on the throat and heart chakras. This will focus the willpower and attune it with emotional intelligence and communication skills.

Turquoise is a color of spiritual compulsion and self-protection. When the green heart and blue throat chakras are combined, one is likely to navigate life from a spiritual standpoint, allowing intuitive personal development to dominate mundane concerns, including job and relationship matters (particularly if these are unfulfilling). By employing these chakras and being aware of the colors thus created, we access the blue vibration of will and the yellow of empathy and compassionate love, which abide together in the form of the green heart chakra. This, of course, is a vernal color appropriate to Iris, a goddess of hope and new life, particularly of light after darkness.

Iris is a functional archetype quick to be of use to gods and humanity alike. In invoking (or convoking) her, we may access the more humanitarian and self-disciplined traits of the human psyche. As Iris is simple and straightforward, so is our means of accessing her.

Visualization for Improved Communication Skills

After you have showered and meditated for a while on your throat and heart chakras, combine them in your mind's eye, surrounding yourself with green and turquoise light; refresh yourself with a little spring or mineral water, and envision your entire body glowing white. At its center, from the tailbone up to the top of your skull, is an elongated spectrum of red, orange, yellow, green, blue, purple, and violet-white. Hold this vision along with a sense of your causal purity.

Now envision the Goddess of the Rainbow in her robes of white, swift-footed as she casts her arc of gentle all-healing light across the sky. One by one, transfer each color of her rainbow into the relevant power point along your spine, neck, and skull; as you do, concentrate on the qualities engendered by this benefactress, as follows:

Root chakra: Envision this root area bathed in a powerful red light. Feel the health and vitality of your being, the cleanliness of your blood as it circulates, and your ability to interact with others as the driver of a healthy, active human vehicle. It helps us live in the present, earthed and rooted in our incarnations.

Intestinal chakra: While you contemplate the orange ray and spin it in with your own orange chakra, concentrate on your charisma and ability to get on with others from all walks of life and at all levels of experience. Also, be aware of your faculty of discrimination.

Solar plexus chakra: Concentrate on the pure, compassionate, yellow light emanating from the center of Iris's rainbow and connect it with the center of your spinal column, just beneath the base of the sternum. Think of your positive points as an individual being and consider how good a friend you are. If you have hang-ups or doubts in this department, now is the time to clear out your negative feelings to make way for the new, positive approach. Focus bright yellow light on this chakra and send it energy until you feel socially confident and aware of your integrity as a companion and friend.

Selfishness should be consciously eliminated from your criteria in attracting and sustaining friendships; it is not a person's position or physical manifestation that counts, but the essence of their interaction with you. This may sound obvious, but it is sad and surprising how many habitual liaisons considered to be friendships are essentially corrupt once the surface is scratched. Purifying the solar plexus chakra will help purge such negative influences. If you are unsure of somebody's motives in wishing to spend time with you, imagine them attached to your solar plexus by a cord (as, indeed, they are), and send bright yellow and white energy into it for as long as you feel inclined.

The state of the cord when you first imagined it will speak volumes. If it was golden, strong, or straightforward, fine; but if frayed, dirty, or otherwise unpleasant-looking, you can imagine the sort of influences it is channeling. Also, its reaction to the positive energy you sent it will tell you a great deal, while simultaneously influencing the relationship in real terms on the astral plane. If it actively absorbed the light and appeared healthy afterward, you may deduce that your own positive qualities can maintain or even redeem that relationship; if it reacted badly to the light—in a worst-case scenario, it actually dissolved—you may conclude a case of good riddance to bad rubbish.

Cleansing yourself of negative and vampiristic influences can only help improve your balance and aid the maintenance of a healthy core of inner energy. A cleansing fireball of yellow light will help achieve this goal.

Heart chakra: The color of growth and abundance permeates your heart, inviting new emotional interactions and the flourishing of affections. Consider the integrity of your emotions, your ability, like Iris's, to distinguish between affections received or imposed, and those that comprise a genuine response to beings of a higher nature or those spiritually resonant to you. In addition, imagine a center of white light in this area, indicative of your physical health. Visualize it glowing brilliantly in conjunction with the vibrant green of your heart chakra.

Throat chakra: As you envision this spinning sky-blue discus, imagine lines of thin blue light entering and exiting your throat. These are communication cords, vibrating with the sagacious guidance of your particular spiritual gurus and protectors. Everybody has spirit guides of some sort, though these may not be evident as specific personalities or entities. It is mainly through the throat chakra that they access our systems and make their voices audible to us.

Chapter 15

As you soak up the blue of Iris's rainbow and incorporate it into your shining astral aura, bear in mind that you are servicing your capacity to receive higher information and, consequently, should find it easier in the future. Of course, the more care you lavish on your psychic radio, the more efficiently it will work and the easier it will be to transmit from it. By concentrating sky-blue light into your throat area, you are improving your fluency in the divine language, not to mention your ability to translate and speak it. This is a good way to cut any nonsense from your dialogue; you will soon find yourself saying only what you mean and avoiding what you don't.

Third eye chakra: As you incorporate the final violet streak of Iris's rainbow-light into your system, it causes your forehead to glow a bright purple; resolve to balance your spiritual side with your physical condition on a day-to-day basis. Iris, as Temperance, represents the reconciliation of all elements of being; like her, you will not forget one in deference to another.

Imagine brilliant white light flowing in through your crown chakra and running down your spine via your third eye area. As it hits each glowing color zone it intensifies the light. The tip of your skull becomes white, your forehead vibrates violet, your neck is an airy sky-blue, your heart is a brilliant green, your solar plexus glows like sunlight, your stomach is bright orange, and your root chakra a startling red. The light flows down and up, balancing and replenishing your energy in every extreme of your body. Let it fill outward until it touches the tips of your fingers and flows from your toes with nothing lost; your energy is seemingly limitless.

Feel the balance; the calm knowledge that this is how it ought to be; this is the original and pure state. Your history means nothing except the progress made to bring you to this point; you are now fully empowered to enter your future with confidence in your own abilities and diplomatic skills.

Repeat this exercise whenever you feel in need of a spiritual refresher, or when you simply wish to reharmonize your life with your environments: physical, mental, and spiritual.

GLOSSARY

Akasha: The fifth element, spirit—along with air, earth, fire, and water—represented in the West as the tip and surrounding circle of the pentacle. In the East it usually takes the form of a purple or black egg, symbolic of all knowledge.

Amrita: A celestial potion; the Hindu equivalent of ancient Grecian ambrosia. This sweet drink could confer immortality, and was the cause of many struggles between gods, devas, and asuras—the angels and demigod demons of Hindu mythology.

Asana: A yogic posture, seated in particular.

Astral body: In Western terms, the third body (after the physical and subtle), relating to emotion, dreams, and creative inspiration. The layer most related to the chakras in the physical body, and which can permanently transmigrate after death. It is usually the vehicle for astral travel.

Beltane: May Day, the most fertile and green of the sabbats. A powerful and positive current in the Western Hemisphere.

Bhakti: Devotional worship and homage. Lovingly tending and offering to the gods.

Bindi: In Hinduism, the spot of red, detoxifying tumeric or *kumkum* traditionally placed between the eyebrows/around the ajna chakra. Can also denote marriage or religious adherence (being married to the Divine). A decorative feature emphasizing focus on the third eye, it has also enjoyed popularity in the West.

Casting a circle: A circle is cast before magickal rites, usually by invoking the quarters in turn, each of which represents a particular element and point of the compass. The caster traces the circle in the air or on the ground and strongly envisions this area blessed and protected by the elements and concomitant spirits, and free of negative influence. Once it is cast, the circle becomes a sphere of protection and anonymity (if desired) in which to freely perform magickal activities. It is sometimes helpful to cast a swift circle prior to a tarot reading or visualization: it also serves to focus one's attention and to enhance psychic perceptions. At the end of the activity, the circle can either be deconstructed or left to fade on its own, though it is not usually passed through while still in operation. See also *Quarters, invoking* for further details.

Causal body: The finest of the body-sheaths, relating to the highest principles of individual and cosmic existence.

Chakras: The numerous energy hubs on the body/bodies; variously described as wheels, whirlpools, and discs of light. These centers distribute life force throughout the psychospiritual and physical systems. They are key to yogic techniques and can be utilized in visualization and magick as keys to specific traits and aspects of the self, as well as to engender particular qualities. The seven major chakras are detailed in the introduction.

Dharma: The Sanskrit name for the principle of cosmic order. The code of conduct of the individual that safeguards integrity and ensures longevity of the soul. Virtue and the upholding of sacred law. In nature, the balance and sustenance of the universe.

Etheric body: In Western terms, the layer of aura between the physical body and the astral.

Ghee: Clarified butter ubiquitous in India; often of a particularly rich yellow color. It is used in offerings, lamps and candles, and as a religious smearing-substance during festivals such as Holi, the street-and-temple carnival in which multicolored paint-powder is showered on all as a symbol of joy, spring, love, Krishna, and Radha.

Gita Govinda: A twelfth-century tract depicting the story of Krishna and Radha in the form of a pastoral play.

Higher Self: The sure, still voice within; the witness or *drashtuh* of the Yoga Sutras; the part of the constitution rooted above mundane concerns and ephemeral emotions. The overseer of incarnations; the wise guardian of the individual; this is the part of us most conversant with cosmic energies, and most relevant when approaching deities and lateral beings. One interpretation is that the Higher Self is the part of the immortal soul it is most easy to communicate with; another is that it is the archetypal expression of one's essence garnered during countless modes of being—a psychospiritual average mean. It is not a manifestation of the singular subconscious; it is *both* coherently accessible and independent of the body, though it helps to fashion the physical self and its attributes. However, the definition is by nature subjective, and there are arguably as many forms of Higher Self as there are individuals. In this book, the term is used to indicate the spirit-self with which it is possible to communicate and the side of us that represents the sum of our wisdom, insight, and clarity of vision.

Ka: Along with the ancient Egyptian *ba* and sometimes *akh*, part of the soul. The ka survives after death and can even reside inside a statue of its owner's body, or, more usually, inside the mummified one. Meanwhile, the ba flies free and, through reunion with the ka, eventually finds its way to the underworld via the Halls of the Assessors.

Kali Yuga: In Hindu philosophy, the present age; the last of four whose traits have degenerated as they progressed. Ours is an era of strife, ignorance, and discord, in which mantric meditation is purported to be the chief path to redemption. The Krishna and Gayatri mantras, for example, are said to counteract the effects of the Kali Yuga when chanted.

Kama: Hindu god of love; equivalent to Grecian Eros/Cupid. Also, the qualities of desire, love, and pleasure; along with wealth and prestige, one of the chief lures of this plane. Kama can be granted by Lakshmi, and it is the sole pursuit of Radha and Krishna.

Kundalini: In yogic philosophy, the coiled, primal energy rooted at the base of the spine but capable of ascension through the chakras to create states of bliss and union with the divine. Essentially feminine in nature, the kundalini shakti is an essential part of the ascension process of reintegration with Source. Particularly related to the great Hindu ascetic god, Shiva.

Leela: A play of dualistic reality in which actors demonstrate spiritual matters through symbolism.

Mataji: Honored Mother; an Indian term applied to benefactresses of all kinds, including divine.

Matrikas: Little Mothers; the seven gruesome clones of Kali and/or Durga who help them in battle.

Moksha: In Hinduism, liberation from mundane existence, to which most of us aspire. Also, beauty; a gift bestowed by such beneficent deities as Lakshmi.

Navaratri: Nine nights and ten days spent twice a year—usually March and October—in honor of Durga in her many forms.

Paramahansa: Literally, supreme swan; the title given to elevated spiritual masters (such as Paramahansa Yogananda) with reference to their transcending of earthly matters. Like the swan, they glide on the murky waters of this realm, their purity undefiled. Also, a celestial swan used as a mount by such deities as Lakshmi and Saraswati.

Patrata: In Hinduism, fitting oneself to be a suitable vessel for the divine through self-discipline, mental and physical fitness, fasting, austerities, good habits, and general worthiness. It is essential, however, to retain a humble attitude and not to flaunt one's spiritual attainments.

Prana: The "breath" of life; sometimes visible as fast-moving globules of energy; usually construed as yellow in color. This energy can be consciously assimilated into the body, particularly through visualization and breathing techniques. There are several different types of prana, including the cosmic, and five physical varieties.

Prema: Selfless love, as exemplified by Radha for Krishna.

Puja: Sanskrit word for worship and giving of gifts and attention to the deities. This can be private or communal. In India, the celebration or festival of a particular god or goddess, sometimes lasting a number of weeks.

Quarters, invoking: When casting a circle, the entities representing the elements are invoked, along with the elements of air, fire, water, and earth themselves. Each of these quarters is stationed at a particular point of the compass, the most usual correspondences are: air and East, fire and South, water and West, and earth and North. The practitioner provides the fifth element, the Akashic principle, by connecting to this through the Higher Self, and the circle becomes a microcosmic universe in which all matter is contained. The magick or ritual activity is then performed with the Lords of the Elements and various protector spirits or deities standing guard against unwanted influences.

Ras: The sacred, sensual dance of Krishna and Radha, or a representation thereof.

Sabbat: There are eight major sabbats, all of them agricultural in origin and based on the seasonal tides of the Old World (predominantly Celtic regions). Often referred to together as the Wheel of Life or the Wheel of the Year, these festivals represent crucial points in the tides of earth energy and allow for contrasting modes of magickal work. Sabbats are also celebrated on the full moon, or at the nearest possible time before one (esbats). The energy of the sabbat is usually harnessed and used for specific purposes. The major celebrations are: Imbolc (February 1), the Spring Equinox or Ostara (March 21), Beltane (May 1), the Summer Solstice or Litha (June 21), Lammas or Lughnasadh (August 1), the

Autumn Equinox or Mabon (September 21), Samhain (October 31), and the Winter Solstice or Yule (December 21).

These dates are based on the British seasons; they should *really* be judged by planet, plant, bird, and beast, not a calendar. The sabbats are also celebrated on the eve before or at the nearest full moon when their energy is particularly strong.

Samhain: The Celtic celebration of October 31, when the emphasis is on death, drawing inward, latent cycles of continuity, and the eternity behind the veil of physicality. It is a time of easy interaction with other planes of existence.

Samsara: The soul wandering in the cycle of material life and delusion—known as maya—divorced, or seemingly so, from Source. The ordinary state of mundane, materialistic, socially encumbered, egocentric human consciousness.

Satya Yuga: In Hindu philosophy, the first of the four (all exceptionally lengthy) ages; the Golden Aeon of Truth and Closeness to God; indeed, the opposite of this one. It equates roughly in its symbolism with the Western Lemurian Era.

Sekhem: Originally meaning "scepter," a modern-day school of healing allegedly based on ancient Egyptian, Lemurian, and even Sirian practices.

Shakti: In Hindu mythology, a feminine consort and power; the female aspect of the Cosmic Intelligence, embodied by the wife of Shiva. The term also refers to an active energy and strength sometimes confused with—but distinct from—a *siddhi*.

Siddhi: A psychic power attained through yoga and hardship, often looked down upon by Hindus as a vanity whose core power ought to be channeled to higher ends such as enlightenment, rather than "spent" on such tricks as levitation, psychism, wrestling tigers, manifesting gems or *vabhuti* (holy ash) and the like. Nevertheless, siddhi are a sign of potent powers gained.

Sistrum: A musical instrument that produces a jingling metallic sound, also used to ward off evil. It is particularly associated with Hathor and Isis.

Solarization: The process of imprinting a substance such as water with the properties of, say, color or gemstones, by subjecting it to strong sunlight in conjunction with these properties. See Introduction for further details.

Tapasya: The performances of hardships, self-discipline and meditation in order to evoke inner fire for spiritual transformation. Through this, one can ask boons of the gods and gain *siddhi* powers.

Vedas: Amongst the primary scriptures of Hinduism, consisting of the *Rig Veda*, or hymns to the gods; the *Samaveda*, or priests' chants; the *Yajurveda*, or magickal prose; and *Arthavaveda*, or mantras and chants. There are many subcategories, of which the Upanishad philosophies are probably the best known. Other texts are also of vast significance, especially the *Bhagavad Gita*, derived from the *Mahabharata*, the epic philosophical poem ascribed to Vyasa.

Vina: A four-stringed Indian instrument not unlike a diminutive sitar; enjoyed by many deities, particularly Saraswati.

Viraha: Love in separation, such as that evinced by Radha for Krishna.

Vratas: In Hinduism, tasks or penances performed with a particular goal in mind, usually during the festival or in the temple of the deity specific to that goal.

Wicca: A populist form of religious modern witchcraft, reestablished in differing forms by Gerard Gardner and Alex Sanders in the UK around the 1960s, now widely spread into numerous subcategories. This form of nature worship, combined with aspects of British folklore, Western Mystery traditions, and individual spirituality, appeals to many whose spiritual lifeblood has been drained by orthodox religions and contemporary modes of living, and who prefer a Goddess-orientated/inclusive, or gender-balanced religion to the more conventional options.

Yantra: The Hindu system of sacred geometry in diagram-form; used in association with a mantra to activate its properties. Often they serve to represent the true essence of a particular god or goddess. Yantras, like spells, may be designed to cover every conceivable desire, from protection to progeny to spiritual liberation.

Yoga: Usually translated as "divine union," but perhaps best described by Paramahansa Sri Nithyananda as "not a drop entering into ocean, but the ocean entering the drop." The practice is composed of physical, mental, and spiritual disciplines that make the union possible and thus lead to self-realization, such as opening the third eye or ajna chakra through mantras and meditation. The primary forms of yoga are:

Bhakti: Yoga of devotion. It includes chanting the names of God(dess) in mantras, offering to the deities, developing a sense of personal connection with the Divine.

Jnana: Yoga through knowledge. It involves an intellectual probing of one's own existence as well as significant knowledge of the Vedas, and lateral mental disciplines.

Karma: The yoga of right action. Working selflessly toward good with no desire for reward either here or in the afterlife.

Raja: Also known as ashtanga yoga, raja yoga is an autonomous path involving eight major "limbs" of yoga, or disciplines of mind, body, and soul, based on the Yoga Sutras of Pantanjali.

BIBLIOGRAPHY AND
RECOMMENDED READING

Armour, Robert A. *Gods and Myths of Ancient Egypt.* Cairo: The American University in Cairo Press, 2005.

Ashcroft-Nowicki, Dolores. *The New Book of the Dead.* London: Aquarian/ Thorsons, 1992.

Atreya. *Prana: The Secret of Yogic Healing.* York Beach, ME: Samuel Weiser, 1996.

Beckman, Howard. *Mantras, Yantras & Fabulous Gems: The Healing Secrets of the Ancient Vedas.* New Delhi: Balaji Publishing, 1997.

Bernard, Theos. *Hindu Philosophy.* Mumbai: Jaico Publishing House, 1989.

Bhaktivedanta, Swami Prabhupada. *Bhagavad Gita as It Is.* Los Angeles: Bhaktivedanta Book Trust, 1986.

———. *The Perfection of Yoga.* Los Angeles: Bhaktivedanta Book Trust, 1984.

Bly, Robert, and Jane Hirshfield. *Mirabai: Ecstatic Poems.* Boston: Beacon Press, 2004.

Bonds, Lilian Verner. *Colour Healing.* London: Vermilion, 1997.

Brennan, Barbara Ann. *Hands of Light*. New York: Bantam, 1988.

Budge, E. A. Wallis. *The Book of the Dead*. London: Routledge & Kegan Paul Ltd., 1956.

Burkert, Walter: *Greek Religion: Archaic and Classical*. Cambridge, MA: Harvard University Press, 2013. Originally published 1977.

Butler, W. E. *Apprenticed to Magic*. London: Aquarian Press, 1990.

———. *Magic & The Qabalah*. London: Aquarian Press, 1990.

Cannon Reed, Ellen. *Circle of Isis: Ancient Egyptian Magic for Modern Witches*. Newburyport, MA: New Page Books, 2002.

Clark, Rosemary: *The Sacred Magic of Ancient Egypt*. St. Paul, MN: Llewellyn Publications, 2003.

D'Este, Sorita. *Circle for Hekate; Volume 1: History and Mythology*. Avalonia, 2017.

———. *HEKATE: Keys to the Crossroads*. London: Avalonia Books, 2006.

D'Este, Sorita, and David Rankine. *Hekate Liminal Rites: A Historical Study of the Rituals, Spells, and Magic of the Torch-Bearing Triple Goddess of the Crossroads*. London: Avalonia Books, 2009.

Dharma, Krishna. *Beauty, Power and Grace: The Book of Hindu Goddesses*. San Rafael, CA: Mandala Publishing, 2017.

Farrar, Janet, and Stewart Farrar. *Eight Sabbats for Witches*. London: Robert Hale, 1984.

Faulkner, R. O. *The Ancient Egyptian Book of the Dead*. London: Guild Publishing, 1985.

Fortune, Dion. *Moon Magic*. London: Society of the Inner Light, 1995.

———.*Psychic Self-Defence*. London: Thorsons, 1995.

———. *The Sea Priestess*. Northamptonshire, UK: Aquarian Press, 1989.

Frazer, Sir James. *The Golden Bough, A Study in Magic and Religion*. Abridged version. Hertfordshire, UK: Wordsworth Editions, 1993.

Bibliography and Recommended Reading

Grant, Joan. *Eyes of Horus*. London: Corgi Books, 1975.

———. *Winged Pharaoh*. Toledo, OH: Ariel Press, 1987.

Grant, Kenneth. *Hecate's Fountain*. London: Skoob, 1991.

Graves, Robert. *The Greek Myths*. London: Folio Society edition, 2003.

———. *The White Goddess*. London: Faber and Faber, 1961.

Harrison, Jane. *Themis: A Study of the Social Origins of Greek Religion*. London: Merlin Press Limited, 1963.

Harshananda, Swami. *Hindu Gods and Goddesses*. Madras: Sri Ramakrishna Math, 1987.

Hesiod. *The Theogony*. Translated by Hugh G. Evelyn-White. First published 1914.

Homer. *The Iliad*. Translated by Robert Fitzgerald. Oxford, UK: Oxford University Press, 1984.

Houston, Jean. *The Hero and the Goddess: The Odyssey as Mystery and Initiation*. London: Aquarian/Thorsons, 1992.

Ions, Veronica. *Egyptian Mythology*. Middlesex, UK: Paul Hamlyn, 1968.

Kinsley, David. *The Goddess' Mirror: Visions of the Divine from East and West*. Albany, NY: State University of New York Press, 1989.

———. *Hindu Goddesses: Vision of the Divine Feminine in the Hindu Religious Tradition*. Delhi: Motilal Bersidass, 1987.

Knight, Gareth. *The Practice of Ritual Magic*. Albuquerque, NM: Sun Chalice Books, 1996.

Lang, Andrew. *The Homeric Hymns*. New York: Simon & Schuster, 2017. Originally published 1899.

Larousse. *The Larousse Encyclopaedia of Mythology*. Edited by Robert Graves. London: Paul Hamlyn, 1964.

Lemesurier, Peter. *The Healing of the Gods: The Magic of Symbols and the Practise of Theotherapy*. Dorset, UK: Element Books, 1988.

Bibliography and Recommended Reading

McLeish, Kenneth. *Myth*. London: Bloomsbury, 1996.

Morgan, Mogg. *Tankhem: Seth & Egyptian Magick*. Oxford, UK: Mandrake of Oxford, 2012.

Mumford, Jonn. *A Chakra and Kundalini Workbook*. St. Paul, MN: Llewellyn Publications, 1995.

Nithyananda, Paramahansa. *Living Enlightenment*. Mumbai: Life Bliss Foundation, 2009.

Paglia, Camille. *Sexual Personae: Art and Decadence from Nefertiti to Emily Dickinson*. New Haven, CT: Yale University Press, 1990.

Patanjali, Maharishi. *Yoga Sutra*. Translated by Dr. Omanand. Indore: Paramanand University Trust, n.d.

Penczak, Christopher. *The Witch's Shield: Protection Magick and Psychic Self-Defense*. Woodbury, MN: Llewellyn Worldwide, 2010.

Prabhavananda, Swami, and Christopher Isherwood. *Bhagavad-Gita: Song of God*. Madras: Sri Ramakrishna Math, n.d.

Rankine, David. *Heka: The Practises of Ancient Egyptian Ritual and Magic*. London: Avalonia Books, 2006.

Rietveld, James. *Artemis of the Ephesians: Mystery, Magic and Her Sacred Landscape*. New York: Nicea Press, 2014.

Scully, Nicki. *Sekhmet: Transformations in the Belly of the Goddess*. Rochester, VT: Bear & Company, 2017.

Sharman-Burke, Juliet. *The Mythic Tarot Workbook*. London: Rider Books, 1989.

Singh, Jodh. *The Wild Sweet Witch*. London: Philip Mason, Penguin, 1947, 1988.

Trobe, Kala. *Invoke the Goddess*. St. Paul, MN: Llewellyn Worldwide, 2000.

———. *Invoke the Gods*. St. Paul, MN: Llewellyn Worldwide, 2002.

———. *Witch's Guide to Life*. St. Paul, MN: Llewellyn Worldwide, 2003.

Versluis, Arthur. *The Egyptian Mysteries*. New York: Arkana, 1988.

Vivekananda, Swami. *Hanuman Chalisa*. Madras: Sri Ramakrishna Math, undated.

Wills, Pauline. *Colour Therapy*. Dorset, UK: Element Books, 1993.

Yogananda, Paramahansa. *Autobiography of a Yogi*. Los Angeles: Self-Realization Fellowship, 1990.

———. *The Divine Romance*. Los Angeles: Self-Realization Fellowship, 1992.

Zaehner, R. C., editor and translator. *Hindu Scriptures*. London: Everyman, 1992.

Referenced or Recommended Websites/Channels

Arsha Bodha Center on YouTube

Author's own website: www.kalatrobe.com

Covenant of Hekate: www.hekatecovenant.com

Hecate lecture at the Hekate Symposium, Glastonbury 2014, by Melissa Harrington; Oracle Television UK on YouTube

Hindu Academy on YouTube—for a more traditional approach to the subject of devotion to Hindu deities, and Vedic philosophy

Kundalini Yogini on YouTube

Thinking Allowed and New Thinking Allowed with Jeffrey Mishlove on YouTube

Bibliography and Recommended Reading